Our Kindly Parent—the State

OUR KINDLY PARENT —THE STATE

The Juvenile Justice System and How It Works

PATRICK T. MURPHY

The Viking Press | New York

First published in 1974 by The Viking Press, Inc.
625 Madison Avenue, New York, N.Y. 10022
Published simultaneously in Canada by
The Macmillan Company of Canada Limited
SBN 670-53111-1
Library of Congress catalog card number: 73-19322
Printed in U.S.A.
Second printing October 1974

Frontispiece photograph
by Charles Harbutt (Magnum)

For my parents, Arthur and Eileen Murphy,
and for my grandfather Patrick Kelly

THE COURT: *Do you want to go home?*

THE WITNESS: *Yes, Sir, I want to go home. Everyone wants to go home. They ain't never allowed it.*

THE COURT: *Are you tired?*

THE WITNESS: *I've been tired for the longest.*

FOREWORD

THIS BOOK attempts to explain the juvenile justice system as seen through the eyes of a lawyer litigating in that area. As an advocate for my client's rights, I have taken one side of the issue in the courts, and I suppose my thinking has been colored by their tribulations.

From what I have seen, the child welfare and juvenile justice systems do much more harm than good. This judgment is based upon five years of constant litigation in every tribunal from the United States Supreme Court to the lowest municipal court in Chicago against the various bureaucracies which make up the juvenile justice system.

In writing this book, I have attempted to set forth the facts as they occurred, accurately and chronologically. Most of the events described here were obtained during the investigation of cases which ultimately were litigated. Only in a few places have I purposefully confused the chronological order of the events, and then only to shield the identity of the children and families involved. I have changed the names of all the children and families whom we represented and who are named in this book, but the names of other individuals have not been changed.

Since the inception of the juvenile courts almost a century ago, a veil of secrecy has surrounded them and their activities. The alleged reason for this secrecy is to protect the names and lives of the children and families who are "aided" by the juvenile justice system. But, as I shall point out in this book, the secrecy is perpetuated more to protect those who work within the state bureaucracies than to maintain the anonymity of those who are compelled to endure being "saved" by the system of juvenile justice. This book was written in an attempt to pierce that veil of secrecy and privacy, and to enlighten the public about how in fact our nation "saves" children and their parents.

ACKNOWLEDGMENTS

It is impossible to acknowledge and thank all the people whose toil contributed this book. In a very true sense, I have merely chronicled what I have seen within the juvenile justice system and what I and others have been involved in. It is hard to acknowledge all of the others. However, this volume certainly could never have been written without the dedication and legal insight of Lewis A. Wenzell, John D. Shullenberger, James M. De Zelar, Clara Ann Bowler, and Christine Dove. Besides these, the work of Roger Derstine and Joan Levin, two lawyers who joined our staff as this book was going to press, must be acknowledged. I thank also the various social-work students, law students, and others who worked part time as investigators and researchers, and who contributed not only to our lawsuits but to this book: Margaret Avery, Barry Barnes, Susan Dahl, Arlene Earlebacher, Gail Hamity, Sarah Johnson, Patti Jostock, Jerome Kleijunas, Fredrika Miller, Mary Murphy, Carol Murray, Susan Ptacek, Marlene Safferstein, Sana Shtasel, Nancy Tarlow, and Mike Thompson. And I must thank and acknowledge the work of Theresa Williams, Bennye Clay, and Margaret O'Dell, who in the face of deadlines, under the threat of tyranny, and under impossible working circumstances typed and turned out briefs, memoranda of law, threatening letters, and other important legal documents.

I should like to thank the man who hired me, Arthur Young, and his successor, Kenneth Howell, for allowing us the independence to litigate against sacred cows and standing by us when pressure was put on them to do away with our office. Lastly, I wish to thank Elisabeth Sifton, of The Viking Press, without whose patience with, and suggestions to, a novice author, this book could never have been written.

It would be prostitution to attempt to acknowledge and thank the people whose unfortunate stories and lives make up the grist of this book. Almost from birth, we have sentenced them to lives of material and emotional deprivation. I hope that, in some small way, this book will stand as a monument to their own tolerance, patience, and understanding of us who have too readily condemned innocent people to hopeless lives.

P. M.

Chicago, Illinois
September 1973

CONTENTS

Foreword | vii

Acknowledgments | ix

1. June 1970: The Beginning | 3

2. Runaways and the Courts | 16

3. Restraints and Rehabilitation | 32

4. Care, Custody, and Maximum Security: Our Battle in State Courts | 46

5. Care, Custody, and Maximum Security: Our Battle in the Federal Courts | 72

6. The Demise of Maximum Security | 93

7. January 1972: We Revise Our Strategy | 102

8. Detention Centers and Mental Homes for Sane and Nondelinquent Children | 108

9. How to Dump Homeless Children in Out-of-the-Way Places | 133

10. The Family-Saving Quagmire | 148

11. Looking Back and Looking Forward | 164

Appendix | 180

Our Kindly Parent—the State

1

June 1970: The Beginning

In 1870, a fifteen-year-old Chicago boy named Daniel O'Connell was arrested and charged with being "destitute of proper parental care, growing up in mendicancy, ignorance, idleness or vice." He was placed in an institution where, according to the same statute, he was to be "disciplined, instructed, employed and governed" until he either was reformed or reached the age of twenty-one. Apparently, Daniel had spent much of his time on the city streets, and there is some indication that he had turned to Oliver-Twist-type exploits. His mother had abandoned him and the rest of the family, and his father was not properly disciplining him. A lawyer became interested in the boy's case and filed a writ of habeas corpus in the Illinois Supreme Court, seeking the boy's release. The Illinois Supreme Court did release Daniel, and the judge's opinion stated:

> It cannot be said that in this case that there is no imprisonment. This boy is deprived of a father's care; bereft of home influences; has no freedom of action; is committed for an uncertain time; is branded as a prisoner; made subject to the will of others and thus, feels that he is a slave. Nothing could more contribute to paralyze the youthful energies, crush all noble

> aspirations, and unfit him for the duties of manhood. Other means of a milder character; other influences of a more kindly nature; other laws less in the restraint of liberty would better accomplish the reformation of the depraved and infringe less upon inalienable rights.

This decision was considered quite illiberal by the child- and family-rescuers of the day. It obviously hindered them from saving from their undeserving parents the children growing up in the immigrant ghettos that were so much a part of the nineteenth-century American city. What was even worse, the Illinois Supreme Court had looked behind the statute and into the realities of the institutional life and in effect was saying that the discipline meted out to O'Connell was, in fact, imprisonment.

By the turn of the century, the *O'Connell* decision had been almost completely eroded. Social reformers had pushed slowly but irrevocably for a court of their own to deal with the problems of juveniles and their families—specifically, poor juveniles and poor families. The first juvenile court in the United States was set up in Chicago in 1899. Hearings were supposed to be informal and nonpublic. Records were confidential, and children were detained not in adult prisons but in facilities of their own. A new vocabulary was improvised to symbolize this new social order. There were no criminal complaints filed against the children—merely petitions. There were no warrants—only summonses. There were no arraignments—but hearings. There would be no juries and no real trials. There was no need for lawyers, because there were no adversaries, inasmuch as the mutual aim of everyone involved was not to contest, object, or even seek the truth of the charges against the juvenile and/or his family, but simply to treat the juvenile and his family, regardless of guilt. Today, there are courts like these in every American jurisdiction.

According to acts and statutes that have set up this system, the juvenile court is only to serve as a vehicle by which the state assumes the role of a kindly and understanding parent toward errant children and incompetent families. Incarceration of juveniles is not allowed. The state, through the juvenile court, simply determines what is in the best interests of the child and his family and provides accordingly. The first section of most juvenile court acts usually states that its purpose is (I am using the language of the Illinois statute here) "to secure for each minor . . . such care and guidance, preferably in his own home, as will serve the moral, emotional, mental and physical welfare of the minor and the best interests of the community; to preserve and strengthen the minor's family ties whenever possible." The act goes on to state that when it is necessary to remove a child from his family, the state must provide "custody, care and discipline as nearly as possible equivalent to that which should be given by his parents."

The juvenile court and the custodians and guardians to whom the courts remand a child have custody over him until his twenty-first birthday. So a child convicted at the age of ten of an offense such as petty theft may be kept under the watchful eye of his kindly parent the state until his twenty-first birthday, whereas an adult convicted of the same offense may receive at most a penalty of six months in jail.

When a child is convicted of an offense and his removal from society is deemed necessary, he is not imprisoned with a correctional agency but, instead, committed to a Youth Commission or a State Juvenile Correctional Division—where, of course, he may not be punished. He is sent not to a jail but to a training school or camp where he learns from his kindly parent the state how to lead a good life. There are no "cells" but "rooms," and there are, naturally, none of the accouterments of adult prisons such as facilities for solitary confinement.

The Illinois Juvenile Court Act is similar to most others in separating children's offenses into several categories. Acts that would be criminal if committed by an adult are termed delinquencies. But, since the emphasis in the juvenile court is on treatment and rehabilitation rather than punishment, juveniles are much more readily convicted of a technical offense than an adult would be. For instance, I was once present in court when a seven-year-old youngster was pleaded guilty by the public defender for throwing a stone at a neighbor child. (He missed.) Children caught committing offenses such as running away from home, truanting, breaking curfew, or simply disobeying their parents are normally placed in a bracket called "person in need of supervision," "minor in need of supervision," or "incorrigible." In Illinois, the term "minor in need of supervision" is used. And, lastly, a minor allegedly living in an environment injurious to his or her welfare may be adjudicated "neglected" and taken from his or her parents.

A child adjudicated either a "minor in need of supervision" or "delinquent" in Illinois could be placed under supervision, put on probation, or be committed to the Department of Corrections —that is, until 1973, when new legislation prevented the commitment to the Department of children not convicted of criminal acts. If a child is adjudicated "neglected," he or she is usually taken from the parents and placed under the guardianship of a state agency. In Illinois, that agency was until 1969 either the Department of Children and Family Services or the Children's Division of the Department of Public Aid, but in 1969, the two merged into the Department of Children and Family Services.*

The Juvenile Court of Cook County is located in an industrial, grimy area on the near West Side of Chicago, about ten minutes on the expressway from the Loop. The neighborhood originally was a part of the Taylor Street Italian ghetto in which Saint Frances Cabrini and Jane Addams labored and from which sprang, along with thousands of good citizens, Al Capone. A few

---

*For purposes of simplicity, the two earlier agencies will be identified throughout this book by the name of their successor agency, the Department of Children and Family Services (DCFS).

blocks of that Italian ghetto still remain, but Mexicans are slowly displacing the Italians as the latter move to the western suburbs. The Chicago campus of the University of Illinois is located about a mile to the east. That campus, which was built several years ago, played no little part in breaking up the ethnicity of the formerly Greek-Italian neighborhood of small homes and shops. A black ghetto extends from the Court east for about two miles and west to the city line five miles away. The area immediately around the Court is populated with small factories belching black clouds, so the neighborhood seems grimy even on the brightest days.

The Court itself, a three-story, sooty gray building, is the nation's largest juvenile court, and in it more than 26,000 petitions are handled annually. Behind it looms a similar building, the Arthur J. Audy Home, a detention center for children awaiting trial who must be incarcerated because it is "in their best interests."* The outside of the Juvenile Court building and the Audy Home are reminiscent of the public-works buildings built during the Depression, but they actually date back to the 1920s. On the inside, the Court looks the way police courts look everywhere. On the usual day, the benches that pack the halls are filled with frightened-looking young children, seemingly defiant and swaggering teen-agers, harassed and poorly dressed parents, modish social workers, and timid witnesses. Actually, the benches hold only about a fifth of the people who come to the Court each day. The rest are milling around, talking, arguing, and, in general, creating a crazy-quilt patchwork of the left-behinds of urban society. The frightened youngsters, swaggering teen-agers, and their parents and relatives are mostly black and brown, with some shabbily dressed whites thrown in. There are a few well-dressed, middle-class white couples whose children may have been charged with possession of drugs or running away from home.

*A new Court building and Audy Home were completed in the autumn of 1973.

The social workers are mostly female, young, pretty, unmarried, and white.

On an average day, about seventy new cases appear on the Court's docket. Besides these seventy, there are probably 200 additional cases on the various judges' calls, up for the second and third time after postponements obtained by one or both lawyers. Also up for disposition are cases of youngsters who have already been adjudicated delinquent, neglected, or in need of supervision, for whom the judges must decide what to do.

Most of the delinquency cases heard initially by the Court result in "admissions." (Since guilt is not assessed in the juvenile courts, there is no question of "guilty" or "not guilty" pleas, but merely of "admissions" or "denials.") These "admissions" are normally accomplished after a two- to five-minute conversation between a college student who is employed by the public defender's office and the parents of the child. The juvenile defendant has little to say. His guilt or innocence is in fact seldom the issue, and if his alleged offense is insignificant, he will simply be put on probation or under supervision. There is theoretically a difference betweeen probation and supervision—probation being a period of supervision after an "admission," supervision being a period of supervision after a "denial." But this difference tends to be more metaphysical than real, and in practice the two amount to the same thing: a court record that will cause the child further punishment the next time he appears in court, perhaps eventually jail.

Since there are so many cases to be heard, the nine judges hearing them are under great pressure either to hasten trials into summary, ten-minute affairs or to talk the attorneys representing the children into pleading them guilty in exchange for probation. Since the public defender's office is run by the chief judge of Cook County, putting pressure on that office is not too hard, and since there were and are no juries to act as a buffer against judicial unfairness, the lawyers representing the children and families are virtually at the will of the trial judge. On a hot uncomfortable day, or on a day when the judges are in a hurry to get away to the golf links or the political clubhouse, it can be hard indeed to receive a fair, unhurried trial. Now if a judge makes a bad decision on either the facts or the law, an attorney can take a variety of legal actions, not the least of which is an appeal to a higher court. But by mid-1970, the public defender, who represented well over 90 per cent of all children in the Juvenile Court, had never appealed a juvenile case, and the Legal Aid Society had appealed only one. With no juries and no appeals, the judges were virtually free of any control over their decisions. Social workers, probation officers, and other social-agency workers had equal freedom, because there was no neutral force overseeing their work. To make matters worse, the Juvenile Court Code called for secrecy in juvenile proceedings so it was just about impossible to know what was going on inside the juvenile bureaucracies.

In most cities, several agencies deal with juveniles. One usually deals with neglected children (in Illinois, it is the Department of Children and Family Services), one with mental-health problems (in Illinois, the Department of Mental Health), and one with children convicted of delinquencies (in Illinois, the Department of Corrections). There will also be hosts of private, allegedly nonprofit agencies—originally set up by churches, for the most part—which the state pays to care for nondelinquent and nonproblem children in foster homes and institutions. (If a child becomes a discipline problem while with these private agencies, it is not uncommon for him to be "traded in" to the state for another, more "suitable" child.)

Despite the excellent goals of the original reformers and the lofty language of juvenile court codes, the simple fact is that after seven decades, juvenile courts are a failure. The juvenile courts have deprived children of procedural safeguards and have taken away their liberty. And the reason for the lack of legal protections was the very theme that was considered at the heart of the system's liberality: that the juvenile court was not to penalize anybody, but only to act on behalf of the state as a kindly parent. However, as the Presidential Commission on Crime pointed out in 1968, "In theory, the juvenile court was to be helpful and rehabilitative rather than punitive. In fact, the distinction often disappears, not only because of the absence of facilities and personnel but also because of the limits of knowledge and technique. In theory, the court's action was to affix no stigmatizing label. In fact, a delinquent is generally viewed by employers, schools, the Armed Forces—by society generally—as a criminal. In theory, the court was to treat children guilty of criminal acts in noncriminal ways, in fact, it labels truants and runaways as junior criminals."

ACROSS THE STREET from the Juvenile Court in Chicago is a crumbling two-story building on the top floor of which is a union hall. Beneath the union hall, in an enormous barnlike space with open pipes and chipping paint, subdivided by plywood semi-walls, is the Juvenile Office of the Legal Aid Society of Chicago. It once housed a store-front church, which has since moved on to greener, and I hope more ventilated, pastures. The front of the office is one huge plate-glass window, and there are no windows that can be opened anywhere in the entire office. When you come into the Juvenile Legal Aid office, you enter a large room, where three secretaries are wearily trying to type coherent petitions and briefs from jumbled tapes. The offices for the lawyers and the social worker (when there is one) are separated off by the plywood dividers which go approximately a half of the way to the sixteen-foot ceiling. The cacophony of typewriters, classical music from an FM radio, conversations quiet and loud—and sometimes obscene—along with the usual give-and-take between members of the staff, are endured by everyone, and the hubbub is compounded by the hum of two air conditioners, whose only discernible effect is more noise.

In June 1970, I was offered the job of chief attorney of the Juvenile Legal Aid Society. At the time I was in private practice, but I had been interested in the Juvenile Court for several years, and in 1969 I had spent about six months representing indigent and neglected youngsters who had been incarcerated at a pretrial detention center for delinquents. After visiting the office, talking to the lawyers who were working there, and mulling over the offer, I told the Director of the Legal Aid Society that I would accept—but only on certain conditions. He would have to let me bring on my own staff, get a decent copying machine, workable dictating equipment, and an adequate legal library. Lastly, and most importantly, he would have to let me cut the case load drastically. He accepted these proposals, and in June 1970 I went to work.

I quickly transferred the lawyers on the staff to other offices and hired Lewis A. Wenzell, an attorney with whom I had worked before and whom I respected as one of the best appellate lawyers in Illinois, and Christine Dove, a social worker. Lew had a master's degree in criminal law, and though he had practiced extensively in criminal trial and appellate work, he knew nothing about juvenile courts. This is exactly what I wanted, and when I hired two more lawyers in 1972, John D. Shullenberger and James M. De Zelar, I made certain that they had the same type of background.

There was a special reason why I wanted this new blood in the office. Both the prosecutors and the public defenders who practice in juvenile courts are often young and inexperienced, and they are easily seduced by the "best interest of the child" mystique that permeates the juvenile bureaucracies. The lawyers end up not questioning what happens to the child after the court determines that it is "in its best interest" to be taken from his parents, or placed in a mental institution, or committed to the Department of Corrections, or put in a foster home. I was determined to avoid this powerful tendency to go along with the system.

I was also struck by the incredible statistic that while hundreds of children were sent by the Juvenile Court to correctional facilities, mental health hospitals, foster homes, and "charitable institutions" every year, the public defender's office of Cook County had *never* appealed a juvenile case. Nor had that office ever sued the state or private agencies over some of the abuses which caused children to be neglected by their state-appointed guardians. Although part of the reason for this was the inexperience of the public defender's lawyers and their simply not knowing how to use appellate and federal remedies, the principal reason was that the lawyers had come to believe, like their counterparts within the juvenile bureaucracies, that once a decision was made to send Johnny or Mary to X placement or Y institution "in his best interests," indeed the child's best interests had been served. When we appealed our first case within two months after Lew and I took over the office, and when we filed our first federal court action a month thereafter, the shock waves in and around the juvenile bureaucracies were unbelievable. Everybody—from lawyers in the public defender's and state's attorney's offices, to the social workers in the juvenile agency—looked upon us as ogres for challenging such a benign system.

It was accident and not design that of the four of us lawyers, only one, Shullenberger, was married. But it became my conviction that *too* many people employed in and around the juvenile-court quagmire, whether they were parents or not, were devoted "lovers of children." The aroma of love, compassion, and best interests permeates juvenile courts. Everything that is done to each child is accomplished in the name of this love. "This hurts me much more than you but it is in your best interests."

I remember once I questioned a social bureaucrat about his decision to send a fifteen-year-old "neglected" child to one of the juvenile prisons. The boy had been orphaned at the age of five and had been a ward of the state ever since. In the year preceding his incarceration, he had run away from several charitable institutions and had slapped a guard at the pretrial detention center.

The Department of Children and Family Services requested that the court send him to the Department of Corrections for the slapping incident. When I asked one of the workers about his motives for this decision, his response was the usual rationalization: it was in John's best interest, because of his need for "proper control." He followed this up by telling us how much he loved children and how he would never harm them. And then he ended by accusing us of caring more about legal principles than children, or else we would recognize that John *did* require the controls that only jail could give him.

After we took over the running of the Juvenile Legal Aid Society, we turned away many requests for legal representation that previously would have been taken. Since we referred these cases to the public defender, the children did not go without legal representation. But we received a great deal of criticism from judges and other lawyers for cutting our case load, and much of it was well deserved. On many occasions, we turned away from our office extremely needy and deserving clients, and I am certain that as a result some families were separated which should never have been and that some children who were either innocent or had committed insignificant offenses were sent to prison. In general, the cutting of our case load probably made for a small increase in the suffering endured by the thousands of people whose "best interests" are served by the juvenile bureaucracies. But the choice was between continuing to represent hundreds of individual clients over the years, doing a marginally somewhat better job at it than the public defender's office, or concentrating on a few cases, doing them as well as we possibly could, and trying to bring about changes that might make the system better for those people unfortunate enough to have to go through it. As it was, we seldom worked less than a twelve-hour day and normally worked part of each day over weekends.

Of course, we could have kept the same long hours representing many hundreds of individual clients in the Juvenile Court, but it is simply impossible to do such a large volume of court-room representation *and* meaningful appellate work at the same time. We did represent clients in the Juvenile Court, but we gradually cut our case load from approximately twenty-five cases a day between the two of us to perhaps twelve cases a week between the three of us. The rest of the time we worked on federal and appellate cases and, later, spent long hours on investigation of Illinois' three child-saving agencies. Although we did cut our case load we did not concentrate on what is sometimes called law-reform cases—taking one or two cases and hoping for a big appellate decision that will serve as a precedent. I felt that too often these cases did little to reform bureaucracies but served mainly as ego-boosting devices for lawyers. We termed our practice Alinsky law—using a variety of legal actions (some valid, some spurious), investigations, and intelligent use of the media to try to move, embarrass, and change bureaucracies.

During our first weeks on the job, Chris, Lew, and I outlined areas which we felt required immediate attention, and began to litigate in them. Among problems we focused on were: 1) the incarceration of children for running away from home; 2) the separating of children from poor parents on "neglect" charges, when, in fact, the parents were merely indigent and not really neglectful; and 3) certain procedural defects in the court system, such as the refusal of the Court to inform parents and children of the consequences of an "admission" of guilt, and refusal of the public defender's office to appeal cases.

One problem which we did not foresee, but which we happened upon in one of our first cases, was the state's practice of discriminating against unwed fathers. In Illinois, as in most other states, there is no such thing as common-law marriage. Therefore, if a man and a woman have lived together for a long period of time and the mother dies, the father has absolutely no right to his children. Under some circumstances the state would simply leave the situation be, but at times welfare agencies become involved, objecting to the way the father was raising the family.

If this happened, they would simply take the children away, without giving the father a legal hearing. At least a wed mother and father had a right to a day in court if the state wished to take away their children, but an unwed father had absolutely no rights to any hearing, since he was considered not only not a parent but as having less rights than a parent. This was made clear by Illinois Supreme Court decisions interpreting Illinois state law. One case, decided as late as 1971, held that an unwed father had no right even to visit his children.

One of the first cases we took on concerned a man named Peter Stanley, who had lived with the mother of his children for eighteen years without marrying her. When she died, the state, not liking his attitude toward them, had taken the children away. Since he was not legally the father, he was not entitled to a hearing to determine whether he had indeed neglected the children. Stanley asked us to appeal the case, and we filed briefs in the Illinois Supreme Court. That Court held that the statute was not a violation of Stanley's equal protection rights. They in effect held that there was reason to discriminate against unwed fathers because they were usually bad fellows. We filed a petition for certiorari in the United States Supreme Court, and to our surprise the Supreme Court accepted the case. During much of late 1970 and 1971, we spent our spare hours preparing briefs for our oral arguments in Washington.

From my earlier experience in representing indigent, neglected juveniles in 1969, I thought I knew the more oppressive abuses within the juvenile justice system. I was certain that, within a year or two, we could confront and attempt to resolve these problems through litigation. But as the hot, muggy summer of 1970 merged into one of Chicago's fine autumns and then into another blustery winter, we kept uncovering additional abuses and more complex legal issues. Working on juvenile cases was like picking up a damp, flat rock and finding thousands of slimy, crawling things under it.

2

Runaways and the Courts

About a hundred years ago, my grandfather, at the age of fifteen, left his father's farm on the west coast of Ireland, got a job as a seaman, and after several years of working on ships, emigrated to the United States. His story is no different from that of millions of other teen-agers who immigrated from all parts of Europe to the United States in the late nineteenth and early twentieth centuries.

Just this year, a sixteen-year-old girl Diane Marcus was kept in a detention center in Chicago for more than a month, simply because she had left home after her parents beat her up for dating an eighteen-year-old boy whom they did not like. In all jurisdictions of the country, children who have committed no crimes are being incarcerated because they are "incorrigible," or "runaway," a person "in need of supervision," a "minor in need of supervision," or because they fall under one of the several other classifications employed to lock up children who are not acting the way their parents or a social worker believe they should.

The laws calling for the incarceration of so-called incorrigible children in order to save them were first enacted in the mid-nineteenth century, probably as a result of the cities being clogged with recently immigrated children who were not attending school and who could not get jobs. In Illinois, the state Supreme Court declared these laws unconstitutional—in the 1870 opinion of *O'Connell* v. *Turner* which I cited in Chapter I. Although the laws allegedly provided for the "safekeeping" of the child, they in fact did nothing more than imprison him for a longer time than an adult could be jailed for a minor criminal act. "Such a restraint on natural liberty is tyranny and oppression," said the Court. "If, without crime, without the conviction of any offense, the children of the State are to be thus confined for the 'good of society,' then society had better be reduced to its original elements, and free government acknowledged a failure."

After the child- and family-"savers" had eroded this decision, Illinois laws again called for commitment of incorrigible youths. Throughout the twentieth century, Illinois courts upheld the provision, and in 1970, exactly 100 years after the *O'Connell* decision was handed down, the Illinois Supreme Court again squarely faced the issue. In the case of *People* v. *Presley,* involving an adolescent ward who "had consistently disobeyed her foster parents and had, in violation of specific rules given her by them, absented herself from the foster home without their consent," she was jailed. In upholding the statute, the state supreme court held,

> We perceive no constitutional infirmity in legislation allowing the adjudication of delinquency and commitment of minors to the custody of the Youth Commission [now Department of Corrections] for misconduct which does not amount to a criminal offense. To hold otherwise would substantially thwart one of the salutary purposes of the Juvenile Court Act, *viz.,* to provide for the rehabilitation of delinquent minors at a stage before they have embarked upon the commission of substantive criminal offenses. The state, as *parens patriae,* clearly has an interest in safeguarding the lives of delinquent minors, as well

> as preserving an orderly society, and it would be largely hamstrung if it were precluded from depriving incorrigible minors of their liberty in the absence of the proof of their commission of substantive crimes.

Under Illinois law, a child may be charged with being "a minor in need of supervision" for such acts as absenting himself or herself from home without permission, curfew violations, truancy, and, in general, being ungovernable—whatever that means. This is not a criminal conviction, and incarceration does not follow a finding of guilt. The child is placed on probation, but if he or she violates the probation by acts similar to those which originally caused the finding of "minor in need of supervision" or other acts, then (until 1973, anyway) the child could be convicted of violating a court order and placed in the Department of Corrections. An "ungovernable" child, in other words, was given two bites of the apple. In practice, he was normally given more than two bites and a judge would not commit a "MINS" minor to the Department of Corrections until after the third violation.

Children sent to correctional institutions as "minors in need of supervision" generally fell into two sometimes overlapping categories. The larger group consisted of adolescents, mostly girls, who could not get along with their parents and left home overnight or for several days—usually to stay with girl friends, but sometimes with boy friends. According to some psychiatrists working at the Juvenile Court, well over half of those who left home under such conditions were not at fault. The parents made unreasonable demands on their daughters, who responded not irrationally by leaving a sick situation. The parents called the police, who eventually arrested the girls. Normally, they were pleaded guilty by a court-appointed lawyer who conferred not so much with the client as with her parents. The child was then placed on probation.

For girls, sexual activity was often considered a violation of probation. Boys on probation did not have to worry about this consequence of promiscuity. But, like many other matters in the juvenile courts, the concern about sex was not explicitly acknowledged. It took me a while to learn precisely what was what. I had been in criminal law for several years and was accustomed to the practical, descriptive terms used in criminal courts, and to the way an indictment charging a person with a criminal offense spells out with great specificity the facts of and surrounding an alleged crime. There never is any doubt as to the nature of the crime, the time, place, victim, and often the witnesses. But things were different in the Juvenile Court, where I sat through hearings for a week, getting acclimated. There were many cases involving girls on probation for running away in which a social worker would tell the judge that the girl had been "sexually acting-out." The judge and the social worker would look at each other knowingly and disapprovingly, and more often than not the girl would end up on the next van to the correctional facility. I was never quite sure what the term "sexually acting-out" meant, but it seemed to cover everything from holding hands to necrophilia. So one day, I went up to one of the social workers and asked what the term meant. "Mr. Murphy," she replied, "these are things that you and I just wouldn't do." As for necrophilia, I agreed. As for holding hands, I made a mental note to exclude her.

The second general group prosecuted under the MINS statute is made up of wards of the Department of Children and Family Services who have been through several foster homes or boarding schools and have been thrown out for behavioral or emotional problems. They may be youngsters of twelve, thirteen, or fourteen who are always getting in trouble and who have been to the Court several times already. The judge either loses patience or simply does not know what else to do with the child.

Shortly after we started working in the Juvenile Legal Aid office, Lew and I were sitting in one of the courtrooms trying to figure out how many kids were being incarcerated as ungovernable and runaways, when the bailiffs brought into the Court a young girl who looked anything but a juvenile. Her case is a good example of a minor who goes to prison because she cannot get along with her parents.

Elenor Miromir was a tall, willowy blonde, wearing a white jersey, a red mini-skirt, and white go-go boots. Her trial was similar to hundreds we had seen in the Juvenile Court, brief and uninquiring.

THE COURT: It's alleged that your daughter violated the terms and conditions of probation by refusing to attend school from April 1 through April 20, 1970, and thereby violated the terms and conditions of probation. At this time both you and your daughter have a right to be present at this hearing to decide whether or not this child has violated probation. Both your daughter and yourself have a right to examine witnesses and cross-examine them and make an investigation of any and all files of the Juvenile Court. Your daughter has a right to remain silent.

Today, you have one of three choices. You can hire an attorney to represent your daughter, if you can't afford one the Court will appoint one free of charge or in the alternative, I'll hear it without a lawyer.

(Whereupon, at this time in the proceedings the Minor Respondent is conferring with her mother.)

THE COURT: Do you want a lawyer, ma'am? Mother, do you want a lawyer?

MRS. MIROMIR: Yes.

THE COURT: All right. Mr. Public Defender, I'm appointing you on this case right now. She was put on probation August 13. Why don't you have her sit down and talk to her.

(Whereupon, the case was passed at this time for a few minutes.)

PROBATION OFFICER: Back on the case of Elenor Miromir.

THE COURT; What about it, Mr. Public Defender?

PUBLIC DEFENDER: There is an admission.

THE COURT: Public Defender appointed to represent minor. Is it stipulated between the State's Attorney of Cook County and the Public Defender representing Elenor Miromir that if the facts were put before the Court it would show that she refused to attend school from April 1, 1970 through April 20, 1970?

STATE'S ATTORNEY: So stipulated.

PUBLIC DEFENDER: So stipulated.

THE COURT: A finding of Delinquency. Violation of probation.

Tell me about this girl.

PROBATION OFFICER: I have been seeing her since, the first of November, 1969, and she was doing fairly well up until the first of March when she stopped attending school. I brought her back into Court on April 7, on a Delinquent Petition for truancy. At that time you extended probation until June 30, and asked for clinical services. In the meantime, she did not attend school and is beyond the control of her mother and we felt that she should be brought back into Court.

THE COURT: What prior station adjustments?

STATE'S ATTORNEY: One station adjustment for running away in March of 1969, for runaway.

THE COURT: How old is she?

PROBATION OFFICER: She'll be sixteen on May 28.

THE COURT: Now, she refused to attend school, is that correct?

PROBATION OFFICER: That is right.

THE COURT: What else does she do at home?

PROBATION OFFICER: Not much of anything, Your Honor, and she has been violating curfew also. [A probation officer has the right to set hours for a minor on probation.]

THE COURT: Have you anything to say, Mr. Public Defender?

PUBLIC DEFENDER: No, Your Honor. I talked to my client and she stated she would continue to refuse to go to school.

THE COURT: Probation revoked, committed to the Department of Corrections, Juvenile Division.

Motion of Probation Officer, probation terminated, case closed on the MINS petition.

Two bailiffs stepped forward, pulled Elenor's hands behind her back, and handcuffed her. Until this happened, Elenor had not realized what was going on, and she burst into tears as they led her away. Ten minutes later I spoke to her in the girls' lockup, a tiny, stuffy cubicle where perhaps fifteen or twenty young girls were in custody awaiting a hearing. Elenor cried incessantly and kept telling me that she could not understand why she had to go to jail when she had never committed a crime.

The trial which sent Elenor to the Department of Corrections, potentially for five years (though, in fact, for one), had lasted only a few minutes and nobody had thought it was necessary to ask Elenor the causes of her actions. More important, no one questioned the mother in an effort to determine whether Elenor's problems were due entirely to herself or whether they might derive at least in part from her mother. Most important, no one thought it relevant to ask whether Elenor was in fact doing anything wrong. At the time of her incarceration for truancy, she was one month short of her sixteenth birthday, at which time it would no longer have been required for her to attend school. Quite obviously, the truancy charge was an excuse for putting Elenor in prison, where she would not embarrass her mother and where her mother wanted her to be. A few months before the hearing I attended, the probation officer had told the judge that the divorce of Elenor's parents had caused much of the distress in her life, and that Mrs. Miromir, who had emigrated from Yugoslavia ten years before, was not in tune with American ways and was in fact treating her daughter as if they lived in a small Serbian village.

Elenor had originally been convicted of being a "Minor in Need of Supervision" about eight months before her commitment to the Department of Corrections. This first conviction stemmed from the fact that after an argument with her mother she had gone away from home for two days and nights which she spent at the home of a girl friend. After that, she did not leave home again, but she did truant from school and got into other trouble. So Elenor was locked up because she did not get along with her mother. No efforts were made by the penal authorities or the Juvenile Court to work with the mother and the girl to attempt to reconcile or counsel them. After three months in the Illinois State Training School for Girls at Geneva, and after we filed a notice of appeal, Elenor was paroled. Almost immediately, she began to date a boy whom she had met through another inmate at Geneva. He was twenty-two years old and black. Elenor's mother objected, and within a few days, the same tensions resurfaced. Several weeks later, Elenor left home, was rearrested and returned to Geneva as a parole violator.

The Illinois Supreme Court later affirmed Elenor's conviction and upheld the constitutionality of the "MINS" law, ruling, as they did in *Presley,* that the state should not be limited in its power to discipline children for noncriminal acts.

Another girl who met a similar fate because of conflict not only with her mother, but primarily with her guardian, the Department of Children and Family Services, was Cathy Beesley. Cathy, a small, unattractive fourteen-year-old, one of eight children living at home with their mother, who was on public assistance, had been involved in curfew violations and one shoplifting incident when her mother was persuaded to admit to "neglect"—this so that Cathy could be helped by the Department of Children and Family Services in order to deter her from a life of extended crime. A caseworker was soon assigned to handle Cathy's case, but, though a Juvenile Court psychiatrist had recommended frequent counseling with the mother and Cathy, the DCFS did not provide it. Within a brief time, they recommended to the judge that Cathy be sent to the penal institution at Geneva, and he followed the recommendation. At the time Cathy was incarcerated, our office did not represent her, but later we did and were able to obtain her release, which infuriated her caseworker, who thought Geneva was an ideal "placement."

One of the principal jobs a caseworker has to do is to find "placements" in homes and institutions for children like Cathy. In this instance, the court psychiatrist and practically everyone else involved agreed that Cathy could not stay at home without counseling. And counseling, they said, was unavailable. So the caseworker had to write to private institutions and find a place for Cathy in one of them. Later we obtained copies of the letters she sent—letters which were, as experts who read them for us agreed, "pure dynamite": no institution was going to touch Cathy after reading them. Now obviously when a DCFS worker attempts to "place" a child, he or she must be honest about the facts and circumstances of the child's case, but it is usual to do this merely by laying out these facts and circumstances. Here is the letter about Cathy:

> Dear Sir:
> We are writing to request your earliest consideration of our ward, CATHY BEESLEY, for acceptance into your residential school program. It is the firm conviction of all who have been working with CATHY that she is in strong and immediate need of a structured, consistent and contained setting which will provide control of her impulse-ridden and aggressive behavior; re-direction of her physical, emotional and mental energies into more satisfying and productive channels, and a support and guidance which will enable her to learn more appropriate

ways of coping with the demands and stresses of her various interpersonal relationships.

CATHY was referred to our Agency by the Juvenile Court for placement planning in July 1970 because of her continued demonstration of destructive, self-punitive and dangerous behavior; and her refusal to accept the routine and supervision of a home situation. Her flights into delinquent patterns of action and re-action had become an intolerable threat and source of intense anxiety to herself, her family and her community.

For a Summary of Background Information, please refer to attached copy of letter to the Circuit Court of Cook County, dated November 11, 1970. You will note that this report details CATHY's case to the point of the Court Hearing on November 12, 1970.

At this Hearing, CATHY and her attorneys were able to persuade the Magistrate to give her yet another chance in the home and community; and on a legal technicality, her commitment to the Department of Corrections was terminated; her Delinquency Wardship terminated, with Proceedings to be CLOSED: and she was released to the custody of the Guardian, and placed with her mother (who once again agreed to try to effect some understanding with her daughter)—until such time as an Institutional placement could be secured.

In the three weeks since her release, CATHY's behavior has only served to strengthen our recommendation for her Institutional planning. From the beginning of her return home, despite her avowals and promises, CATHY has been unable to govern or inhibit her furious outbursts of temper whenever she encounters frustration. She has continued to reject and resist any and all demands made of her, while insisting imperiously that she be gratified by everyone else. Her bullying and physical attacks upon younger siblings and relatives resumed, and with her pervasive self-centeredness has caused increased dissension, turmoil and justified resentment within the family toward her. When questioned or counselled about her actions, CATHY is argumentative, belligerent and highly vocal. In sustained defiance of instructions, she has refused to re-register at school, offering a variety of invalid, illogical excuses. Instead, she leaves the home early, returns late, often after curfew, and persists in association with adults and older adolescents of highly questionable character and activity.

During a recent spirited exchange with her mother, CATHY blatantly asserted her contempt and scorn for all authority figures; and boasted her belief that she successfully fooled everyone at the Court. Further, she announced that she is prepared to use the same tricks again (tears, promises to "be good," little girl act) if necessary to manipulate adults in charge, in order to do as she wishes. Because of the girl's behavior and the attitude reflected in such statements, the mother is in full accord with our planning for CATHY's placement in a more controlled and protected setting. Both she and we feel that no significant change in CATHY's adaptation is possible with her continued placement in her present situation which cannot control her in any way.

You will also find attached copies of recent Psychiatric Evaluation, and materials obtained from the Department of Corrections, which include Psychological Testing Results, Clinical Evaluation, Medical History, and Staff Progress Reports.

Thank you in advance for your review of this referral material. We would be most appreciative of your earliest possible attention to our request that CATHY BEESLEY be accepted for placement in your program. Please do not hesitate to let us know if there are any questions or concerns not covered by the preceding information.

Needless to say, none of the institutions wanted to take Cathy. Within several months, she was back at the Juvenile Court on her mother's complaint that she had been fighting with her brothers and sisters and had violated a 9:30 P.M. curfew. Both the State's Attorney's office and the social worker wanted to get Cathy back to Geneva, but since she had not committed a crime, the only way to do this was to label her a "Minor in Need of Supervision," put her on probation, and hope she would violate the probation. At the start of the court hearing, the social worker told the judge that Cathy would be placed in a foster home but that the state wished to prosecute her for being a "MINS" because of her behavior at home. And from all indications and from the psychiatrists' reports on Cathy, it seemed evident that if she were placed in a foster home, she would run away. We reasoned with the mother and the State's Attorney's Office to drop charges, but they insisted on prosecuting Cathy.

Cathy was convicted in January 1971 for being a "Minor in Need of Supervision." She was put on probation and into a foster home. Within a month, she had run away from the foster home and was placed in the Audy Home behind the courthouse, awaiting trial on the charges that she had violated her probation. On March 1, she was convicted of violating the probation and was incarcerated at Geneva. The trial judge, who was sympathetic toward Cathy but saw no alternative, ordered the caseworker to continue to make every effort to place Cathy in another institution. About ten months later we looked into the case again. Sure enough, Cathy was still at Geneva and the caseworker had made only one or two attempts to place her elsewhere. We filed a Rule to Show Cause why the caseworker and several of her superiors should not be held in contempt of court for violating the order the judge had handed down in March 1971. Eventually, we subpoenaed the Director of the Chicago office of the DCFS and several other supervisors. The judge ordered the social worker removed from the case and released Cathy from Geneva—she had been there almost one year to the day. Of course, she was returned to her mother and, in the meantime, no counseling had been accomplished with the two of them, nor had any efforts been made to work toward achieving a reconciliation. The mother was still living on welfare in the midst of Chicago's West Side slums, still burdened with eight children living at home in a small flat, still in no condition to cope with Cathy's problem. In the meantime, Cathy had received no help in gaining any insights that would help her reconcile herself to her mother and her situation—although she did learn some new things about life which one can only learn in prison.

Elenor and Cathy were not isolated cases. Every year, thousands of youngsters are herded into juvenile courts all over the country simply because they cannot get along with their parents. In the cases that we personally witnessed, and according to knowledgeable psychiatrists, most children who run away from home probably do so for healthy reasons. In too many cases it is the *parents* who need supervision and counseling. Like Cathy, many neglected children are charged with being "minors in need of supervision" by lazy or incompetent caseworkers for whom the Department of Corrections is an easy alternative to hard work and adequate placement.

When we realized that the Supreme Court of Illinois was going to rule against us and affirm Elenor's conviction, we filed a civil-rights suit in federal court seeking to have the incarceration provisions of the runaway statute declared unconstitutional. The plaintiffs in this case were three girls whom we represented and who were charged with violating MINS probation. All three girls were wards of the Department of Children and Family Services. One girl was fourteen, the other two sixteen years old. One was from a poor black family, two from lower-middle-class white families—broken homes, I should say—and one of those had been sexually molested by her stepfather. Each had been adjudicated neglected by the Juvenile Court and placed under the guardianship of the DCFS. One girl had been in four different foster homes in the year preceding our suit and had run away from the last of them.

Although all three girls were intelligent and attractive (prerequisites for getting into private institutions), they had all had sexual experiences and two had experimented with drugs, so the private places weren't interested in them. The Department of Corrections was hence the obvious solution—at least it seemed obvious to their "guardian," the DCFS—and the girls were convicted of being "Minors in Need of Supervision." At the time we got involved in their cases, each had been caught as a runaway or truant, delinquency charges had been brought, and the DCFS was attempting to commit them to the DOC.

While the prosecutions were pending, we filed suit in federal court seeking to enjoin the prosecution and to have the incarceration provisions in the runaway statute declared unconstitutional. In our brief, we pointed out that the institutions to which boys and girls were sent were not significantly different than minimum-, medium-, and maximum-security penal institutions. We remarked that DOC records demonstrated that almost 70 per cent of the girls at the State Training School were there because they had run away from home. Our argument was, essentially, that to imprison children for the act of running away from home was a violation of the Eighth Amendment rights of these children to be free from cruel and unusual punishment.

Our case was assigned to Judge Alexander Napoli, who ruled that there was no federal jurisdiction for it. His ruling was based upon the fact that at the time we filed the suit, prosecutions were pending against the girls, and pursuant to a recent Supreme Court decision orders could not be obtained in federal courts enjoining state prosecutions. But between the time we filed the lawsuit and the time it was dismissed, the DCFS reacted predictably. First, it dropped the three prosecutions, and then it scurried about trying to find private placements for each of the girls—successfully, for they ended up with fairly good private charitable organizations.

But that should not be the end of the matter, we thought. We appealed to the U.S. Court of Appeals for the Seventh Circuit.

They *did* uphold our right to employ the federal court for this type of case, but on the more important substantive question the appeals court did not support our contention.

Their ruling, which does make sense, was that it was not per se unconstitutional to institutionalize a child for running away. But the institutionalization itself could be unconstitutional if it violated the Eighth Amendment's mandate against cruel and unusual punishment. So, if we could show that a runaway was placed in an institution that provided a punishment unequal to the gravity of the so-called offense, then for children at that institution incarceration would be unconstitutional. We were later to use this opinion in cases we brought against various jails in Illinois and the Audy detention home.

When Lew and I had taken over the Juvenile Legal Aid office, we had determined not only that we would use every conceivable legal tool but also that we would employ the news media to help educate the public about the abuses in the juvenile justice system. We made it a habit to give copies of the complaints and petitions we filed to various newspapermen and television commentators. And when a case highlighting the abuses of the system was coming up in Juvenile Court, we would always notify our contacts. When stories about these cases appeared in the newspapers, we were often criticized by the people in the juvenile justice system for publicizing what was going on. They were used to the tradition that juvenile justice proceedings are secret, ostensibly to protect the best interests of the child. That may have been the original intention, but the effect of this secrecy had been to protect the best interests of social workers, lawyers, bureaucrats, and other "child-savers" and "family-savers."

In our civil-rights complaint in federal court concerning the runaway children, we had included an affidavit from one of the three girls, then at Geneva. In it, she had vividly described solitary confinement, homosexual attacks made on her by other inmates, and other routine incidents of penal life. When the suit was filed, all five of Chicago's daily newspapers gave it a lot of coverage, one on the front page, and reporters did later follow-up stories about conditions for runaways at the Audy Home and within the Department of Corrections.

This publicity, along with the pressure from the lawsuits and the good intentions of the new Presiding Judge, the Honorable William S. White, brought about a gradual change in the policy of the Cook County Juvenile Court. As the months went by, fewer and fewer children were sent to the DOC for running away. Those who were, were likely to be victims of the DCFS "what do we do with them now?" syndrome. Eventually, in 1972, the Illinois legislature revised the law so that children could not be committed to the Department of Corrections simply because they had violated a probation placed on them for running away from home. However, temporary detention homes, such as Audy, are still used to teach a runaway or incorrigible child a lesson.

3

Restraints and Rehabilitation

IN THE FALL of 1970, we were very busy preparing briefs on the runaway issue in the Illinois Supreme Court and in federal court, and we were also writing a petition for certiorari in the *Stanley* case (about the rights of unwed fathers) in the U.S. Supreme Court. Besides these appellate matters, Lew and I had a daily case load of about ten hearings each in the Juvenile Court. Added to this, we were still trying to devise a litigation strategy to attack the procedural sloppiness of the Juvenile Court and the various agencies which the Court appointed to care for children.

As was to happen all too often, we were jolted out of these daily appellate and trial labors into a case that for a while absorbed all our time. It involved two youngsters, Billy Armstrong and Tommy Burke, who were in a ward for retarded children at the Elgin State Mental Hospital. That case—and, even more so, one it spawned concerning a fourteen-year-old girl named Matilda McIntosh—highlighted the abuses within the entire system, from the Juvenile Court to the three major state agencies servicing children, and spotlighted certain important problems of so-called rehabilitation. Ultimately, the Armstrong and Burke cases were the subject of two precedent-setting U.S. Court of Appeals decisions.

One bright Indian summer day, I received a phone call from a social worker at the Elgin State Mental Hospital, a facility where retarded and emotionally disturbed individuals were "rehabilitated." It was the first of many phone calls we were to receive from dedicated social workers, caseworkers, guards, counselors, and other personnel who worked long hours and received low pay for trying to do something for Illinois children. Frustrated by the middle-management state bureaucrats who looked the other way when abuses occurred within the system, they would come to us to see if we could do anything about the injustices they observed so often. This time, the southern voice on the other end of the phone identified herself as Carol Klein, and she told me about two boys on her ward who had been tied to their bed in a spread-eagle position for seventy-seven and a half consecutive hours as a punishment for alleged "sexual acting-out." She and another worker at Elgin wanted to come to talk to us about it.

That afternoon, Lillian Kuffel and Carol Klein gave Lew and me a brief sketch of how tranquilizing drugs and restraints were used, abusively they thought, at the Elgin State Mental Hospital. (Restraints are soft ropes used to tie violent mental patients to their beds.) Both Carol and Lillian were attractive, recently married women in their mid-twenties, and it was obvious that they cared a lot for the children they worked with. After their general description, they told us about the two boys, both twelve years old, who had been caught in allegedly homosexual contact in the middle of the night. For this, they were placed in restraints and, with the approval of the Clinical Director of the Children and Adolescent Unit and the Program Coordinator of the ward, kept there for seventy-seven and a half hours.

Billy and Tommy had been spread-eagled to their beds and tied at the wrist and ankle to the head-posts and footposts. They were dressed in short, backless hospital gowns that barely covered their genitals, and during the day their beds were taken from the ward and placed in the dayroom, where the other patients watched television. Although the Department of Mental Health was later to argue that this had been done so that the nurse could keep an eye on them, it obviously caused the boys a great deal of humiliation and public ridicule.

The restraining of the two boys was the last straw for these dedicated young social workers. But there were other forms of "therapy" that distressed them almost as much. For instance, a few days before the restraining incident, Billy Armstrong was made to scrub walls from 7:00 a.m. until about 10:00 p.m. for being, in the words of the DMH log book, "uncooperative and belligerent." This punishment continued on the next day, when Billy became too ill to work. He was allowed to go to bed, but on the following day he again had to scrub walls all day. And for this work he was given only the hospital gown to wear. On another occasion in the same month, Tommy Burke had also been made to wash walls for eleven hours in his hospital gown. Other youngsters were forced to endure similar forms of "therapy."

Within twenty-four hours, we had prepared and filed a civil-rights complaint in federal court alleging that the boys' constitutional rights to the due processes of the law and to be free from cruel and unusual punishment had been violated by the Department of Mental Health. We sought $77,000 in damages for each boy and an injunction against the unreasonable use of restraints. The case was assigned to Judge Bernard Decker, an older judge who had been on the bench for many years. We filed a motion for a preliminary injunction against unreasonable restraints and asked for an immediate hearing.

Routinely, we gave copies of our complaints to the press, and there was a lot of publicity surrounding the case. When we first appeared in court, about a week after filing, I was accosted in the hall by Jerry Goldberg, chief counsel for the DMH. In our conversation, Goldberg referred to Lew and me as publicity-seeking liemongers, but after interviewing his witnesses, he later told us, grinning, that although we certainly were publicity-seekers we weren't liemongers.*

The defense of the medical and supervisory staff at Elgin was that restraints were part of a behavioral-modification program employed to rehabilitate errant youngsters. We were to hear the term "behavioral modification" many times during the next three years, for it was a term used by all public- and private-agency personnel dealing with children to describe what they considered a desirable form of rehabilitation. Broadly and simply, behavioral modification is nothing more than a use of the carrot-stick approach to bringing a person around to one's own way of thinking. If a child does what the staff wants, he is rewarded; and if he doesn't, he is punished. Behavior modification in the hands of experts and professionals is indeed a valid form of therapy. But in the hands of untrained people, as many staff members at Elgin were, it could be dreadful, and in the hands of people who believed that any type of behavioral deviancy should be punished, it was positively medieval. As a result, we saw teen-aged girls locked in "quiet" rooms (a mental-health term for solitary confinement) for weeks on end because they had been caught necking with boys, we saw youngsters in solitary confinement at "boys' schools" because they had hurled racial epithets at guards, and we saw youngsters pumped full of tranquilizing drugs because they had been heard swearing in the presence of women.

A second theory advanced by the DMH to justify the use of restraints was that it was needed to prevent the spread of vene-

*Our relationship with Goldberg over the next three years was excellent, and of all the opponents we had, he was the most honest and candid. He worked very hard to bring about change within the system as soon as he saw any abuses, and, later, when we brought some of the "therapy" that went on within the DMH to his attention, he helped to bring about reform. In several cases where the DMH refused to accept his proposals, he refused to defend it, and they were forced to rely upon other counsel.

real disease. Testifying before Judge Decker, the psychiatrist who headed up the Chicago area for the DMH advanced this theory. Lew suggested to Judge Decker that penicillin might be more effective and less humiliating.

During the initial hearings, Goldberg suggested that we assist the DMH in drawing up a new regulation on restraints. We agreed, and worked with him at writing what we considered a reasonable regulation. The new rule limited the use of restraints to no more than eight consecutive hours, after which restraints could not be used on the same person for another forty-eight hours without the express written approval of the superintendent of the institution. Once a person had been in restraints for two hours, his nearest relatives, attorney, and the superintendent of the institution would have to be notified by registered mail concerning the use of restraints and the reason for their employment.

This regulation was acceptable to us, but we told Goldberg that we would refuse to dismiss the money damages portion of our lawsuit. His superiors in the DMH wanted to withdraw the draft regulation, but Goldberg prevailed upon them not to. (Although Goldberg's motives were as much humane as legal here, this move on his part demonstrated a keen litigation mind which we were not to encounter in lawyers representing the other two major state agencies, Children and Family Services and Corrections.) It appeared that Judge Decker held a conservative view of federal jurisdiction and would just as soon throw the case back to the state courts. There were some grounds on which he could state that no federal cause of action was raised, and that we should employ the state courts. But, with the gross facts of the boys being tied to their beds, it would be difficult for him to do this unless the DMH moved to purge itself. When Goldberg presented the new rule on restraints to Judge Decker, we were forced to admit that the regulation seemed fair and that with it in effect we had no grounds to proceed on our injunctive relief. Still, we argued that the boys were entitled to pecuniary damages for the emotional damage wrought by the state. Judge Decker politely told us to go and use the state court and dismissed the lawsuit, and we equally politely filed notice of appeal in the U.S. Court of Appeals for the Seventh Circuit. We were to wait almost two years for a decision.

Although Carol and Lillian were familiar with the boys' wards at Elgin, they had no idea what went on at the girls' wards. But while I was investigating the case about Billy and Tommy, I encountered a girl whom eighteen months earlier, when I was in private practice, I had been appointed by the Juvenile Court to represent. The girl was a ward of the Department of Children and Family Services, ostensibly because she had alleged emotional problems. But, to my mind, Mary Allen was a very bright girl whose emotional problem seemed to be no more than a sharp tongue that led to her being thrown out of several foster homes because she talked back. Now here she was in Elgin. While chatting with her, we discovered that she herself had been in restraints on several occasions, once for seven consecutive days—for slapping a matron. We expressed shock at this, but she replied calmly. She had not been treated as badly as other girls, she said, certainly not as badly as her friend Matilda McIntosh.

Matilda was about the same age as Mary, thirteen. She also was a ward of the DCFS, and she had been at Elgin for a year, but was now to be found at the Illinois State Training School for Girls, the juvenile prison conducted by the Department of Corrections at Geneva. According to Mary, Matilda had been tied to her bed for twenty-eight consecutive days for striking a matron, and after only two weeks up and about had been put back in restraints for an additional thirty days. She then was prosecuted by the state and committed to the DOC.

Mary's story seemed far-fetched, but we set about investigating it. After checking out records in the Juvenile Court, at Elgin, and with the DCFS, we sought permission to talk to Matilda at

Geneva. Of course, this was denied by the DOC, and we petitioned the Juvenile Court for permission to visit her. This was granted, and I met Matilda for the first time in January 1971.

Matilda was basically a pretty girl, but she seemed to go out of her way to appear slovenly and unattractive. She was overweight, wore her hair shorn off close about her head, dressed in dirty blue jeans, scruffy blouses, and house slippers. She slurred her words and seldom looked one in the eye. But despite all this, Matilda was an extremely intelligent and sensitive person. She spoke easily and well, she could pinpoint time, dates, and names accurately, and she used the vocabulary of a well-educated college girl. She always understood what we were talking about, and unlike almost any other youngster we ever represented, she asked pointed questions about the theory of our lawsuits, about what we were doing and why. She was very finicky and suspicious about our work, and on several occasions told us to delay filing certain briefs and papers until she had time to analyze them more thoroughly. Over the next three years, I was able to build up a relationship with Matilda, and eventually she came to trust me. As Lew and I pieced it together we realized that Matilda's story of her journey through the state juvenile quagmire was one of the greatest indictments of the juvenile-justice system we had ever seen.

Several months before she was born, Matilda's father murdered a male companion of her mother's. He was sentenced to prison for fifteen years for this, and Matilda had never seen him. Her mother struggled to raise her only child alone; they lived in a black ghetto on the Chicago South Side. Sometimes, Mrs. McIntosh went on welfare, but more normally she worked as a secretary. Matilda had no trouble with her work in school, but when she was in the fourth grade, she began to "act out" and cause disturbances in class and in the neighborhood. Given the quality of Chicago public schools, particularly in the ghetto, Matilda's classroom disturbances might have been caused by boredom or by the low and slow caliber of teaching. But the school counselor suggested that the mother and daughter visit with a private social agency and seek family counseling.

For almost a year, Matilda and her mother went to this agency to see a social worker, who finally suggested that Mrs. McIntosh admit to having "neglected" Matilda, so that the state could provide resources for the girl which the mother could not afford. In September 1966, Mrs. McIntosh did admit in the Juvenile Court that she had neglected the child. Of course, she never had, but one must go through this charade in order to receive state assistance from the DCFS.

Matilda was put in an orphanage (where she was the only black child). According to the records of the DCFS, she fought constantly with other youngsters, and the orphanage asked the DCFS to remove her. She was then put in the Audy Home. I shall more thoroughly describe the Audy Home later; suffice it to say here that it was an overcrowded maximum-security institution, originally built for delinquent youngsters, and had only a few recreational and educational facilities. Of course, solitary confinement and other devices were used to keep order at the Audy Home.

Matilda remained at the Audy Home for three months, and in March 1967 was placed in the first of two foster homes she lived in for the next fifteen months. After she got in trouble with the second set of foster parents, she was put back in the Audy Home for another six months. During that time, a psychologist tested her and, in part, observed:

> Matilda's background is one not calculated to develop psychological health. Rejected by her mother, being an only child in this situation, and having a father incarcerated before her birth for murder, do not lend stability to a home. Her symptoms include disturbing behavior at home and school with destructive temper tantrums. She has also been unable to adjust satisfactorily in one placement away from home. Consideration is being given to state hospital placement.
>
> Although Matilda is, indeed, emotionally disturbed, she is

> not psychotic and does not give any basis for commitment to a state hospital.
>
> In spite of her disruptive behavior at school, Matilda does get good grades. This is a reflection of the fact that her basic intellectual ability falls within the superior range, though she now reveals impaired intellectual efficiency, due, primarily, to the emotional disturbance.
>
> Matilda wants so much to be accepted, but the frustration has endured so long she now often works against herself. At best, she tests people to see how they will react to her. At most, she destroys, revealing her anger. Matilda needs to be placed in an environment which is strong and consistent but where the main ingredient is people and not rules. Not only does she need a good, accepting relationship with a woman, however, but she needs to experience an accepting, supportive, but non-threatening relationship with men. Forming a relationship will not be easy because Matilda will not let herself fall for any relationship which is offered. She is, however, a bright girl and people are still important to her. Thus, some leverage is available. In working with her, one must be prepared to accept many frustrations and disappointments without giving up, for she has had to live with many in her life, too.

The case files of children tend to get cluttered up with clinical examinations, psychological tests, IQ scores, caseworker impressions, and tons of other important and not-so-important material. It is always doubtful whether the caseworkers ever review these files, but in this particular case, it is *extremely* doubtful, in light of what happened to Matilda after that report was issued. After being released from Audy in December 1968, Matilda was put in yet another, then a fourth foster home. Finally, in May 1969, Matilda was committed to Elgin State Mental Hospital.

Since Matilda was under the age of eighteen, she was not entitled to a legal hearing to determine whether or not she was actually in need of mental-health care. An adult placed in a mental hospital has a right to such a hearing, but in 1970 children did not. Like the other children in the Children and Adolescent unit at the State Hospital, Matilda was treated by the use of "milieu therapy" and "behavior modification." Milieu therapy generally means that every experience within a ward or at the hospital is meant to contribute to treating the individual. For the most part, the people staffing the ward are untrained and, though some are very dedicated, few really know much about mental-health rehabilitation. Although an institute for juvenile research is funded by the Illinois Department of Mental Health and employs four certified child psychiatrists and other experts, most of the resources for this center go into teaching doctors and social workers who ultimately work in private practice. At Elgin, there were no psychiatrists available to work in the Child and Adolescent unit. The clinical director of the ward was called a psychiatrist but in fact was not. (In Illinois, as in most other states, if a doctor works for the Department of Mental Health for one year, he is then called a psychiatrist for purposes of working within the DMH, but, of course, he may not treat psychiatriatic patients outside it.)

Matilda spent more than a year at Elgin. As time went on, she became more and more frustrated with life there. Moreover, the events of the previous three years had done nothing to lessen the pressures felt by this extremely talented, bright, and sensitive youngster. As with the other inmates, she was given regular doses of tranquilizing drugs. Like Billy Armstrong and Tommy Burke, she was placed in restraints on numerous occasions. Toward the end of her first year, when she got into an altercation with one of the mental-health specialists (matrons) and slapped the woman, she was placed in restraints for almost a month, as her friend Mary had told us. (She was allowed up once a day to shower, but during the rest of the time, was tied to her bed.) She was kept heavily sedated for the initial eight days.

Now restraints, like the quiet room and like tranquilizing drugs, may under some circumstances be legitimate therapeutic aids. When certain patients become so violent that it is necessary to use some means of restraint to keep the patient from harming himself or others, this may be done provided that proper counseling and other forms of therapy are also arranged and carried out. But all too often, in both public and private institutions, such devices are used for the convenience of the staff and not as an adjunct to treatment.

After being released from restraints on the second occasion, Matilda was taken to the Kane County Juvenile Court and prosecuted for the "assault" which had led to her being punished. She was convicted and committed to the Department of Corrections.

In June 1970, she was sent to Illinois State Training School for Girls in Geneva. During her first seven months there, she was kept in solitary confinement on eleven occasions, the longest of which was about a week. As the years rolled by, the administration at Geneva changed and became more benign, and later Matilda spent almost no time in solitary. But she was on the road to becoming an institutionalized person.

In early 1971, after talking to Matilda and verifying the facts in her background we filed a civil-rights lawsuit against the Departments of Children and Family Services, Corrections, and Mental Health seeking $500,000 in damages and a plan whereby the DCFS would guarantee that Matilda would receive therapy for any problems she might have and also pay for her college education. The suit was assigned to Judge Decker, who dismissed it at the same time he dismissed the Armstrong and Burke cases. We appealed, but it was two years before a decision came down —two years which Matilda spent at Geneva.

During the last year, officials of the Corrections Department pressured DCFS more and more often to take Matilda out of Geneva, arguing simply that she did not belong there. If Matilda had had parents, it would be easy to release her in their care, but inasmuch as her legal parent was now the state of Illinois, and since the state refused to do anything for her, she stayed at Geneva. During one of those occasions, we received a court order forcing the DOC to send the girl to a private hospital for an evaluation. That report is in part set out here:

> Matilda McIntosh has been a patient of mine at Presbyterian-St. Luke's Hospital for approximately one month. . . .
>
> She has represented no problem of any kind in management. She has integrated well into the peer group structure of the unit. She has been given considerable freedom, including passes and opportunities to visit friends and family with no difficulties. She has responded to provocative social situations well. I find no evidence of psychosis. While I find some characterological problems, they would not appear to be of such severity as to require incarceration in the case of children from middle-class, or upper-middle class backgrounds. I see large numbers of children with similar pathology on a consultation basis whom I refer for outpatient psychotherapy.
>
> One of the difficulties we face is that a major share of her adolescence has occurred in grossly abnormal and destructive milieu structures. It is quite clear that this girl has needed meaningful relationships to adults, she has needed an opportunity to gradually develop healthy peer group involvement with healthy adolescents, and she has needed an opportunity to explore some life roles for herself. Given her life history and her tremendous feelings of self-depreciation, I feel that it has been extremely unfortunate that she has been put into a variety of social settings in which her role has been one of increased and further depreciation.
>
> While I now feel that she would probably function very well in an open peer group structure, it is clear that she would benefit from some long-term psychotherapy that would assist her to work through some of the trauma of the last few years.

I have carefully reviewed the records of the State of Illinois and am extremely confused by them. I find psychological test material without projective work-ups, I find psychiatric examinations based upon previous histories which are very vague, and it is difficult for me to understand or work out any real plan of management, any diagnostic program, or any clear-cut assistance for this girl within her relationship to the State of Illinois.

While she has done very well at Presbyterian-St. Luke's Hospital and she would probably benefit from a prolonged stay there, and while it is probable that in six months or a year's time we might assist considerably in working through the trauma of the last year, I do not feel that this is the only possible course and there are certainly alternative placements with out-patient care which might reasonably meet her needs.

Might I close by pointing out to you some of the responses of our own personnel to this child since one picks up a great deal by the child and the child's operational dynamics around the responses of the staff of a therapeutic unit. Initially, before she came to Presbyterian-St. Luke's, we only had a history of a child who was called homicidal, dangerous, and destructive. The staff, therefore, anticipated receiving a monster. The monster never arrived. Rather, we got a kind-of frightened, unhappy child, confused, extremely needy, who, at first, was a bit frightened of our own setting, and who took a few days to settle down. Gradually staff became comfortable with her, and she warmed up to staff and staff warmed up to her. Certainly there were some minor problems in interpersonal relationships and some minor provocative behavior consistent with what one sees in adolescents with traumatic family histories, but nothing consistent with a child in need of mental treatment as defined in the Mental Health Code. With the passage of time the staff gradually decided that they were not just waiting for the explosion that must come, but rather, that the explosion was not to come.

In summary, as she prepares to leave us, I am totally confused as to the rationale behind the treatment program of the last six years. Certainly, there is nothing in our experience with her which is in any way consistent with it.

While Matilda's case was still pending in the U.S. Court of Appeals, we filed again in the Juvenile Court seeking an order against the Department of Children and Family Services to provide adequate care for Matilda. Judge White ordered the DCFS to make whatever effort and pay whatever expenses needed to put the girl in the most appropriate placement. Within two weeks, it obtained a placement at Browndale, an excellent private facility for the rehabilitation of disturbed youngsters in Madison, Wisconsin. But Matilda refused to go. All institutions were the same, she said, and since she knew the matrons and other staff at Geneva, and since it was close to Chicago, she would just as soon stay there, where she was somewhat comfortable. Matilda's argument was not exactly illogical, especially for someone who had been so thoroughly institutionalized. And hoping that the Seventh Circuit would ultimately rule in her favor, we did not pressure her to go to Wisconsin.

In the meantime, we tried to get back to our heavy trial and appellate schedule. But those damn slimy things kept crawling out from beneath that rock.

4

Care, Custody, and Maximum Security: Our Battle in State Courts

EIGHTY MILES south of Chicago lies the small farming community of Sheridan, Illinois. Neither here nor in the nearby county seat of Ottawa are black people welcome. If you travel out of the town of Sheridan, down the narrow two-lane country road, you will be surrounded by fields where tall stalks of corn sway gently before the summer's breezes. After climbing one of Illinois' few hills and negotiating a few curves, you will see, in a valley below, one of the institutions built and maintained by the state of Illinois to secure "care, custody and discipline for minors similar to that which a parent should provide." The Illinois Industrial School for Boys, known simply as Sheridan, is ringed by two chained fences, each about twenty feet high, ten yards apart. Rolls of barbed wire cover the top of the second fence, making the institution appear, from the outside, like a Nazi concentration camp.

The Reverend Robert Stuart, an Episcopal priest who in 1971 was assigned to St. Leonard's House in Chicago, an institution for ex-cons, has visited practically every prison in Illinois. Father Stuart, a slender, good-looking man in his early thirties, testified for us in federal court in a lawsuit involving Sheridan:

> As I recall, it is in a valley. You come around a curve, and you could see the whole institution. . . . I remember saying to my companion, "This is just another fortress."
>
> Well, I saw a double fence, and as I recall, the buildings seemed very austere. I seem to remember a building that had that fortress-looking aspect to me . . . that was prevalent thirty, forty years ago in prisons or jails.

Ronald Reed, a guard at Sheridan for four years, admitted on cross-examination during the same federal hearing that Sheridan is a jail. He also gave us a description of the cells at Sheridan. The steel doors on some cell blocks are about thirty inches wide and seven feet high. A small opening is located at eye level, covered by a transparent plastic plate that slides up and down as well as by a steel plate on the outside which locks shut. Each cell contains a triangular-shaped light fixture built into the corner which can be turned off and on only through a control in the gallery. The cell doors are secured by a lock opened by a large brass key. The cellblocks with the solid steel doors have a gallery between the facing rows of cell doors. There is a barred window and a cast aluminum or porcelain combination toilet and sink in each cell. There is only cold running water. A metal bed with a solid cotton or foam-rubber mattress is built into the wall of each cell, and though Reed stated that all boys should have sheets, some do not have pillows. On the solitary-confinement tier, C-7, the boys receive their food on paper plates and use plastic spoons.

All the cellblocks at Sheridan are the same except for C-8 and the dormitory. C-8 differs insofar as the doors are barred instead of being made of solid steel. The side and back walls in these cells are built of concrete, and the barred doors face windows on the opposite wall of the gallery. In the dormitory, there is upholstered furniture, a color television, pinball machines, and a ping-pong table.

About 80 per cent of the population at Sheridan were committed there by the juvenile courts for care similar to that which a good parent should provide, while the remainder were committed by the criminal courts as punishment. The boys were not separated, although those committed by the criminal court tended to attain the honor dormitory more frequently than the others.

Shortly after we lost the *Armstrong* and *McIntosh* cases at the trial level and while we were researching and preparing the briefs for the U.S. Court of Appeals, several women came to our office complaining about punishments their sons had received at Sheridan. Although we knew that abuses occurred in the Department of Corrections, their stories did not seem credible. They told us that their sons had been convicted of such "crimes" as being a passenger in a stolen automobile and running away from home. One of the boys was allegedly retarded. All the boys we were told about had been convicted of delinquencies when they were ten or eleven years old, placed in St. Charles, a medium-security institution, and later transferred to Sheridan, where each had been in solitary confinement for long periods of time. Each of the boys had been given shots of a major tranquilizing drug called Thorazine. We checked the Juvenile Court files and verified the mothers' account of the ages of the boys at the time of conviction. Then we went to Sheridan to interview the boys, and they confirmed the stories their mothers had told us. Several of the counselors at Sheridan substantiated the facts, but would not allow us to use their names for fear they would lose their jobs.

After investigating and discussing the problem for several weeks, Lew and I decided there were probably four constitutional violations and at least one statutory violation arising from the abuses at Sheridan. To begin with, the punishments of protracted solitary confinement and tranquilizers inflicted on boys convicted of insignificant offenses at a young age seemed cruel and unusual punishment in violation of the Eighth Amendment to the Constitution. Briefly stated, when punishment so far outstrips the offense as to shock the civilized conscience, there is reason to believe that the Eighth Amendment's prohibition against cruel and unusual punishment has been breached.

Secondly, it appeared that the rights to equal protection of the laws of at least four of the youngsters whom we represented had been breached by the state. Three of them had been convicted of what would be called misdemeanors under adult criminal law, which carry a maximum penalty of one year in an institution other than the penitentiary. The fourth had been convicted of running away from home, an offense unknown in adult criminal law. These four had been at Sheridan for over a year, and before that at St. Charles for about a year. The boys were thus locked up for two years because there is no felony/misdemeanor distinction in the Illinois Juvenile Code; a child found delinquent remains a ward of the court until his twenty-first birthday. Of course, the reason for this provision is that the child is supposedly being committed and treated, not incarcerated and punished. And if a child does not respond to treatment in the way the correctional authorities believe he should, then he must stay in the institution until he does. This is where "behavioral modification" comes in. We once represented a boy convicted of shooting another boy in the back and seriously injuring him in a gang shoot-out. This wily, street-wise fellow spent only three months at St. Charles before being released, for he knew how to "modify" his "behavior" in order to satisfy the authorities. That is, he knew exactly what he had to do to get out, and he did it. On the other hand, one of the Sheridan youngsters, convicted of running away from home, spent almost a year at St. Charles and more than two years at Sheridan before being released (under circumstances that will appear later). He was not such an expert at "behavioral modification." Our equal-protection argument was simply that once a child convicted of a misdemeanor is locked up for a single moment longer than an adult would be, under circumstances which approached or were worse than those under which an adult would be incarcerated, then the equal-protection clause had been violated. From our experience and from what we could see, Sheridan was worse than most adult penal institutions, and probably as bad as the most maximum-security adult prison in Illinois.

We also felt that the due-process clause of the Fourteenth Amendment had been violated. In general, this clause means that the government must be fair and just in its dealings with citizens, and may not take their property, and punish or penalize them without affording some type of fair hearing. We theorized that the state had made a bargain with juveniles and their parents. Through the Juvenile Court Act, the state in effect said that "we will take away from you [the juvenile and his parents] certain rights which you otherwise would be entitled to. These would include the right to a jury trial, the right to a sentence, the right to bail, and normally the right to appeal. In exchange, we offer you care, custody and discipline similar to that which a parent should provide." Our argument was that once the child and family were compelled to keep their side of such a bargain, then the state was equally bound.

The fourth violation we saw was also a due-process violation. All but one of the boys had admitted his guilt; none had appealed the court's decision. In the 1960s, the Supreme Court had held that before accepting a plea of guilty, the trial judge must warn the defendant exactly what the plea means. He must determine that no pressure has been applied or promises made to the defendant, and that he is admitting his guilt because he is in fact guilty. The defendant must also be informed of the minimum and maximum period of time he may be incarcerated pursuant to his plea. In the Juvenile Court, the judges never tell the juveniles any of these things. In each of our cases, guilty pleas were accepted in circumstances like those in thousands of other cases that come before the Cook County Juvenile Court each year, which I have already described. A hurried conference took place between a public defender or a college-student interviewer and the accused juvenile, and the admission of guilt was automatically entered. The last violation we found lay in the fact that none of the boys had been told of his right to appeal the decision and, if indigent, his right to a free appeal. In adult cases, this is mandatory.

Besides the constitutional violations, there appeared to be a serious statutory abuse. Although it would be practically impossible for the state to provide what the statute calls for—care, custody, and discipline similar to that which a parent should provide—the conditions at Sheridan fell so far short of even a minimum standard of care that it was obvious the state was violating its own statute.

There were several legal actions we could take, and our initial reaction was to file a civil-rights complaint in the federal courts alleging that the constitutional rights of the boys had been violated and hence the need for federal action. But we decided against this because our experience in the *Armstrong* and *McIntosh* cases before Judge Decker had cautioned us that this might not be the most fruitful initiative we could take. We decided instead upon three simple suits in the state court. The first two were petitions for writs of habeas corpus, which we filed in the Circuit Court of Cook County, and which we realized we would lose at that level. The first was on the due-process issue arising from the Juvenile Court's failures to instruct the boys about their pleas and right to appeal, and the second on the grounds that equal protection had been denied. In the first issue, we filed on behalf of one client and argued that he was being detained at Sheridan illegally, inasmuch as he had not been informed of the consequences of his plea of guilty, nor told of his right to appeal. On the second, the equal-protection point, we filed in behalf of four youngsters, stating they were being detained illegally, inasmuch as they had served as much time as an adult would if convicted of the same offense. As expected, we lost both these pleas and filed notices of appeal in the Illinois Supreme Court. We then filed a third complaint in which we alleged that the Illinois Department of

Corrections had violated their duty toward the boys as outlined in the Juvenile Court Act.

This third complaint was assigned to Judge White, Presiding Judge at the Juvenile Court. By the time he heard the complaint, Lew and I had been with the Legal Aid Society for almost a year. During that time, we had raised the mental-health issue, the runaway issue, and the sexual-discrimination issue. Now we were seeking to have a state court look into the policy of the Illinois Department of Corrections. All of these efforts had been innovative and had never before been attempted in the state. The action we filed before Judge White had never before been attempted in *any* jurisdiction. The attorneys from the State Attorney General and Cook County States Attorney's offices were used to laughing off such lawsuits in the state courts, for the judges, appointed by the local political organizations, normally gave them short shrift. In the federal courts, such matters are usually taken more seriously. And after the state had the two petitions for habeas corpus dismissed, the state's lawyers apparently felt that Judge White would dismiss the third complaint as well. However, they misjudged the temperament of the Presiding Judge.

William S. White had been appointed Presiding Judge in the Juvenile Court shortly before Lew and I went to the Legal Aid Society. He was a short, thin, balding man, with high cheekbones and intense eyes. He was the first black judge to supervise a Division of the Circuit Court of Cook County, and, at fifty-six, he had a long and distinguished career behind him. A graduate of the University of Chicago Law School at the age of twenty-one, he had been too young to be admitted to the Illinois Bar. Years of working within the Cook County Democratic Organization and slowly advancing to a position of relative prestige and power, particularly for a black, had made him a cautious person.

The state filed a motion to dismiss all complaints; if granted, there would be no hearing. Evidently so confident that the Judge would dismiss our complaint, the Attorney General's Office did not bother to file any memorandum of law or fact in support of their one-page motion to dismiss. We filed a lengthy memorandum of law, and on the day the motion was to be argued, we brought the mothers of the boys to court to testify concerning the truthfulness of our allegations. Much to the dismay of the DOC and its attorneys, Judge White, after listening to the arguments and hearing some hearsay testimony from the mothers, refused to dismiss the complaint and ordered a hearing to commence within two weeks. When the DOC tried to stall for time, he refused to give it.

The Juvenile Court Building is in one of the slum areas of Chicago and away from the center of town. The huge volume of business it conducts rarely gains the attention of most people in Chicago, and this hearing too went without notice until the final days. Much of the testimony we introduced in court—about brutality, solitary confinement, and what we considered unconscionable use of tranquilizing drugs at Sheridan—never made the papers. Our witnesses, the boys, testified about being put in solitary confinement for up to thirty and forty consecutive days, sometimes even longer. They told of tranquilizers administered as punishment. The state admitted to these actions, but insisted they were legitimate means for psychotherapy. Their two main witnesses on this point were the superintendent of Sheridan and Dr. Smith, a part-time physician assigned there.

Dr. Smith, a short, pudgy man in his sixties, had been employed at Sheridan since 1948, and normally spent two and a half days a week at the institution. He testified that usually the tranquilizing drugs, Thorazine for the most part, were prescribed by him after a nurse gave him telephoned information that had been relayed to her by the guards about the inmates' behavior. The nurse would then administer the drug, unless Dr. Smith were on the grounds, in which case he would do it himself. Dr. Smith testified that Thorazine was used as part of a total treatment program to rehabilitate the boys. When we asked him to enumerate the goals of this program, he said that the superintendent or the part-time psychiatrist would be in a better position to do that than he, his only contact with psychiatry being one course taught to him in medical school in the late 1930s.

The superintendent at Sheridan at the time was Charles Rowe, a big man, over six feet tall and weighing well over two hundred and fifty pounds. When we asked him on cross-examination about the use of Thorazine, he declined to answer, on the grounds that it was a medical decision whether or not to use it —thus throwing the ball back to Dr. Smith. But much of his other testimony was responsive and candid. Solitary confinement and Thorazine, he said, were really the only ways to keep control in the overcrowded institution. He also acknowledged that he had never worked at any penal institution except Sheridan, where he started in 1962.

Later, we put social workers and psychiatrists on the stand to testify that while solitary confinement and quiet rooms used in moderation and with professional assistance could be legitimate means in a psychotherapy program, the manner in which these were used at Sheridan was totally punitive. Toward the end of the hearing, the Chicago newspapers and media became interested in our case and began to publicize some of the atrocities at Sheridan. But from our point of view, it was too late to make any difference. The "heat" engendered by the news stories would not be great enough to bring about the enormous changes that we knew were necessary. On July 9, 1971, Judge White issued an order against the Illinois Department of Corrections. It did not go as far as we could have wished, but it was a radical decision inasmuch as it was the first time that a juvenile court judge had exercised his continuing jurisdictional power over juveniles and issued an order against a state agency. Judge White limited solitary confinement to five consecutive days—except if, in the judgment of the superintendent, it was necessary for the child to remain longer. If this were the case, the child would have to be seen by a psychiatrist, who would have to state in writing that the child would not be harmed by further solitary confinement, and this same psychiatrist would have to give reasons why the child would benefit from such confinement. Judge White also ordered that any inmate receiving tranquilizing drugs would have to be counseled by a psychiatrist within twenty-four hours.

The Attorney General's office immediately filed for an appeal in the Illinois Supreme Court and within several weeks appeared before one of the justices of that Court, asking him to suspend Judge White's order pending an appeal. After hearing arguments for about two minutes, the judge did suspend Judge White's order. On the way out of the Supreme Court chambers, the Assistant Attorney General handling the case grinned impishly at Lew and me. "Better luck next time," he cheered. He knew and we knew that an appeal to the Illinois Supreme Court on this sort of matter could take a year or a year and a half. (As things turned out, it took two.) Apparently, the state felt that since it hadn't been badly hurt by the publicity and since Judge White's order could have no effect for at least a year, they were over the Sheridan problem for the time being. But, Lew and I had not been resting on our laurels either.

As the hearing before Judge White was drawing to a close, Lew and I explored all the possibilities and likelihoods in the case. We correctly surmised that we would probably get a favorable ruling from Judge White but that the rather conservative Illinois Supreme Court (particularly conservative on Juvenile Court matters) would suspend his order pending appeal and might eventually rule against us on procedural grounds. (These grounds would be that a state court trial judge had no right to place an order against a state agency.) So several days before Judge White's ruling, we ourselves went to the Illinois Supreme Court on a petition for an expedited appeal from the trial court's denial of our petition for habeas corpus on the equal-protection issue. If the state Supreme Court did grant us this expedited appeal, it would mean that both we and the state would file briefs and argue the case within several months. If we then received a favorable decision, we speculated, all that would happen would be that the case would be remanded to the trial court for a hearing on the facts. What we really wanted—and what we got, as it turned out—was for the Illinois Supreme Court to deny our motion.

We then pulled another arrow from our quiver. Several weeks after Judge White's order was suspended by the state Supreme Court, we filed a petition for a writ of habeas corpus in the federal court in Chicago on the equal-protection point. In order to file a federal writ of habeas corpus, all state remedies must be exhausted. The Attorney General's office argued before the federal judge who received the case that there was no federal jurisdiction since we had not really exhausted the state appeal remedies. Their argument was that, although our petition for an expedited appeal was denied, we would still get a hearing in the state Supreme Court. But, we pointed out, the state Supreme Court, in denying our motions for expedited appeal, had in fact negated the constitutional rights of the boys. For if, as we alleged, the boys had been denied the equal protection of the laws by spending one second more than an adult could in a maximum-security prison for an identical offense, then every minute the boys spent at Sheridan was a denial of their constitutional rights. We were not surprised when the judge ruled in our favor and ordered a hearing.

DURING the two months until our hearing in federal court started, there was more activity at Sheridan than had gone on in the previous decade. Superintendent Rowe was "promoted" to an administrative job in Springfield. His replacement, David Brierton, had quite a bit of experience within the Department of Corrections, both at the Cook County Prison and at a "model" juvenile institution the DOC operated.* Within the same two months, more than a hundred boys were paroled from Sheridan, and while the hearing went on (for about a month), several more were released each week.

Our petitions for writs of habeas corpus were assigned to Judge James B. Parsons, the only black judge that has sat on the federal bench in Chicago. He was appointed in 1961 by President Kennedy. Judge Parsons is an average-sized man, but his massive shoulders and stocky build made him appear much taller when he presided at the elevated bench in the federal courthouse. I had never tried a case before Judge Parsons, but I had heard some derogatory comments about him made by members of the local bar, who thought he took too much time in pretrial hearings and in trying a case. As the weeks dragged by and our hearing went on and on, we too lost patience with the imposing figure of the Judge, and with his deliberate, methodical ways. But this manner was merely a function of a probing and inquisitive mind. Judge Parsons quite correctly wanted to have all the legally permissible facts available to him before making a decision.

The attorneys representing the Corrections Department managed to antagonize Judge Parsons in every possible way. Both lawyers, during pretrial motions as well as when making objections during the hearing itself, seemed to belittle the Judge, who had after all been sitting on the federal bench for ten years and had served on the state bench before that. I don't exactly

*Valley View, the institution formerly directed by Brierton, is a good example of a benign penal institution. A minimum-security prison, it houses a population of boys who, for the most part, should not have been incarcerated in the first place —youngsters involved in only minor scrapes. Of course, this was true of our Sheridan plaintiffs too, but they had not accepted prison life so readily, and hence "needed" maximum security.

know why they made this tactless mistake, but the chief prosecutor was trying one of his first federal cases and he was accustomed to state judges, who demand little from the state prosecutors (who, after all, are political protégés). Moreover, he realized that we had "sandbagged" him into the federal courts and was irritated; somehow his ire was misdirected at Judge Parsons.

On the day the hearing was to begin, the state made two costly errors. First, the Assistant Attorneys General in charge of the state's defense made the tactless mistake of asking Judge Parsons to excuse himself. It is a very serious matter for a lawyer to ask a federal judge, or any judge for that matter, to excuse himself from a case because of "prejudice," and we did not think the state had grounds to argue that Parsons should. We suspected that the motion had something to do with the fact that Parsons was black, as were three of our four petitioners and 80 per cent of the inmates at Sheridan. The two lawyers who represented the state in the Sheridan case were the best trial lawyers in the Attorney General's office, but, as they later confessed to us, most of their strategy was dictated by Corrections officials. Judge Parsons denied the state's petition, but it unfortunately engendered hard feelings between the Judge and the state's lawyers which lingered throughout the trial.

The state made another blunder which outraged Judge Parsons. At 7:00 A.M., on the first day of the trial, a leather belt with an iron lock in back was fastened around the waist of each of the four boys. On the front of each belt was a steel loop through which handcuffs were placed. The boys were thus handcuffed in such a way that they could not move their hands at all. They were put in a station wagon and brought to Chicago, where they drove around the Loop for a while and then parked in front of a building in downtown Chicago. The boys asked if the straps could be taken off because they were uncomfortable and embarrassed as passers-by gaped at them. But the straps were not taken off until just after noon, when the boys were brought into Judge Parsons' courtroom. The federal marshals there, who were accustomed to dealing with every type of prisoner from murderer to extortionist, never treated federal prisoners in such a fashion, and they were clearly shocked.

In a hearing on a petition for a writ of habeas corpus, there is no jury. The judge rules on both the facts and the law. Since we were the plaintiffs and were asserting that the state had violated the boys' constitutional rights, the burden was on us to present our case first, and to demonstrate that the facts which we alleged in our petitions not only were true but also had harmed the boys to a degree that their constitutional rights were violated. We decided we would meet this initial challenge by having the four plaintiffs and at least one other inmate from Sheridan testify. We also used one or two other witnesses (such as Father Stuart) to shore up the kids' credibility—particularly with the press and other media. Since we theorized that the state's defense would be that the punishments were merely therapy, we decided to save our experts for rebutting the State's case.

The first boy to testify was Larry Woodson, who was sixteen and had been at Sheridan for almost three years. Larry, his twin brother, and a younger sister were raised by their mother in a Chicago Housing Authority project on the near South Side. (This was one of the hundred or so fifteen-to-twenty-story concrete, barracks-like buildings that extend for miles along Chicago's Dan Ryan Expressway). His first arrest was for pulling a false fire alarm when he was five years old. After that, Larry had frequent contact with the police; when he was ten, he was charged with, and convicted of, criminal damage to property (he broke a plate-glass window in a department store). He was placed on probation, but shortly after was incarcerated for ten months at St. Charles as a probation violator. He was paroled, but his parole was revoked when he was thirteen, and he was committed to Sheridan.

Larry was a tall, gaunt youngster, with shiny, copper-color skin and closely cropped hair. He was a rather good-looking youngster but had a twitch on the right side of his face and a very pronounced limp, both of which he claimed were nonexistent prior to his incarceration at Sheridan. The state never attempted to prove that any of his testimony, or that of the other inmates, was false. Indeed, they could not, since Sheridan's records substantiated the boys' stories.

Larry testified that there were two solitary-confinement sections at Sheridan—upper tier C-7 and the back end of C-8, which could "drive a man crazy back there." Upper tier C-7 had the usual solid steel doors and differed from the regular cells at Sheridan only insofar as the boys were not allowed out of them except to shower (between one and three times a week). The administrators of the DOC who later testified claimed that there was no solitary confinement at Sheridan, but that at times boys were "confined to room" as part of a "total treatment" program. (Later, after several court decisions and a spate of bad publicity, the Department introduced a new term called "Reintegration Unit" in which a boy was placed in a cell by himself as part of a "total treatment" program).

Larry Woodson had been in solitary confinement about fifty times, the longest spell for four months. He estimated that he had been in solitary three hundred to four hundred days in all. He also testified that he was given injections of tranquilizing drugs.

> At first they had tranquilizers, you know. It was stronger than the stuff they had recently in the stores. It was real strong. This kind, the first kind, would knock you out about two days. You wouldn't know the days went past. But now the one they got recently will put you to sleep all during the day and keep you up all night. That is about all.

Woodson had been given the drugs about a dozen times by means of injection on both sides of the buttocks. For two weeks, between January 28 and February 10, 1971, he received shots every day. Larry testified that he had been at Sheridan for only two months when he first received shots.

> Some cat hollered out of the window, called this guard, you know, called him a pig, and I guess he thought it was me. He said it was, which it wasn't. The cat was next door. I guess it was him. I don't know who it was but the cat next door hollered it out because I heard him.
>
> Then all I knew, I was laying in my bed reading a book—[the nurse] came up here, told me to turn around, didn't tell me what I was going on shots for, or nothing.
>
> Then I refused. I said, "I am not going to. I don't know what I am going on it for."
>
> Then this—he is a captain now, his name is Steve, and this other guy [guard] Andy, they twisted my arm and tried to break my neck and whatnot, so I just took the shots.

Woodson testified that in the month before testifying he saw a psychiatrist twice, but in the previous thirty-two months he had seen one only twice for only a few minutes.

The drug company which produces Thorazine, in a letter to physicians who use the drug, points out that the ". . . principal use [of Thorazine] is in the treatment of severe mental and emotional disorders. It is a potent tranquilizer." The company warns that "Thorazine should be used with caution on patients with chronic respiratory disorders," and concludes, "The use of [Thorazine] in any non-medical situation is improper and constitutes a serious form of drug abuse." A psychiatrist testified that the use of Thorazine made no sense in the absence of a total psychiatric program.

Besides solitary confinement and Thorazine, another punishment which Larry Woodson outlined was "sets." A "set" is a period of time ranging from six months to two years to which a boy could be sentenced by a "court" consisting of a counselor and a guard. Since children are placed with the DOC for a term not to exceed their twenty-first birthday, to be released only at the discretion of the DOC, this meant the boys could not gain their freedom until they had first served their "sets." The "set," or sentence within a sentence, could be reduced by getting good time. The rules provided that a boy could receive a two-year "set" for "striking an employee, striking and seriously injuring another young man, running or attempting to run, starting a fight resulting in a serious disturbance in the dining room, the TV room, gymnasium or playing field." A one-year "set" could be the result of "yelling obscenities or any type of vulgar language out of a window at anyone. This includes any employee, another young man, any line or other visitor; pressuring another young man to engage in devious sexual behavior; creating a serious disturbance on the gallery; fighting or creating a disturbance in any area of the institution where a group of young men are assembled; throwing hot shoe polish on another person." According to the same rule, an inmate could receive a six-month "set" for "intentionally breaking windows; marking on or drawing pictures on any walls of the institution; shouting or whistling at visitors or employees, particularly female visitors or employees; intentionally destroying state property of any type description; sniffing glue, paint thinner, gasoline, etc."

Our other complaining witnesses in turn testified to long periods in solitary confinement, Thorazine, and other punishments.

Earl Lasser, the lone white among the four—he looked like a sixteen-year-old Howdy Doody, and had just the slightest trace of a southern accent—according to psychiatric reports functioned intellectually between retarded and dull-normal, whatever this is. Earl was no genius, but he didn't seem retarded to me. He was raised with his six brothers and sisters in Uptown—a hillbilly, American Indian, and Puerto Rican ghetto on Chicago's North Side. He was nine years old when he first began to get in trouble with the police, and he was arrested for truancy, running away from home, breaking a window, shoplifting, curfew violations—the usual. He was brought to the Juvenile Court, and a psychiatrist there concluded that Earl was on the road to behavioral disturbance unless some type of intervention was obtained. The psychiatrist suggested a school with strict controls and therapy. Earl's father was in prison, and his mother, who was receiving $307 a month for herself and her seven children, was in no position to get Earl into a private boarding school. A social worker advised the mother to agree to a finding of "neglect" in the Juvenile Court, and to transfer her parental rights to a state agency. We had already learned that this recommendation was all too frequently made to poor parents whose children required certain types of psychiatric or psychological assistance. Anyway, Mrs. Lasser did admit that Earl was neglected, and the Department of Children and Family Services obtained guardianship. Earl was left with his mother while the DCFS continued the case on nine different court appearances over twenty months, each time explaining to the judge that they were trying to get different living arrangements for Earl. In the meantime, DCFS did nothing in the way of private or public therapy to assist Earl with his alleged problems. Finally, the agency asked the court to dismiss their guardianship, since they were unable to find a suitable boarding school for Earl. The court agreed.

Within several months, Earl was in trouble again and brought back to Juvenile Court. Another psychiatrist saw him, and gave a report identical to the earlier one. Again, his mother was talked into admitting to "neglect," and Earl was once again placed under the guardianship of the DCFS. Several times, he ran away from the foster home he was put in in order to return to his mother. In June 1969, he was arrested with several other boys as a passenger in a stolen car, which he claimed he did not know was stolen. The public defender pleaded Earl guilty, and within a month he was on his way to the Department of Corrections and incarcerated in St. Charles, at the age of thirteen, for the first time in his life. He ran away from *this* new home seven different times, on each occasion returning to his mother. Mrs. Lasser dutifully sent Earl back to St. Charles, but in September 1969 he was finally transferred as a security risk to Sheridan.

Earl had been at Sheridan for twenty-two months at the time of the trial, and he estimated that he had been in solitary confinement for over three hundred days. The Sheridan records showed that during the first fifteen months he had been in solitary for 262 days. The reasons given for this were generally that he had behaved badly and that "it was in his own best interest." On December 9, 1969, for example, Earl received six days of solitary confinement for disrespecting his teacher. He was back on the seventeenth for four days, for talking in class. Later, a psychiatrist testified that initial periods of solitary confinement, particularly when they are not justified, tend to snowball and may cause the inmate to act even more aggressively, thus inciting more punishment. Earl made it through the Christmas holidays before he was again locked up on December 28 for "ranking" (pounding on his cell door), knocking out glass, and attempting to fight. He remained in solitary confinement until February 2 because of offenses which he committed while in solitary. According to the Sheridan records, these were again "ranking" and being loud at his window, tearing up a sheet and faking suicide, and smearing shoe polish about his cell and himself.

Earl was released from solitary but found himself back within a day for being "loud on the gallery." This lasted until mid-March—with the principal event occurring on February 27, when he attempted suicide. For this offense, he was kept in solitary an additional two weeks and was given Thorazine for ten (according to his testimony) or seven (according to the records) days. Not once during this incredible period of time was Lasser seen by a psychiatrist.

James Thompson, his younger brother, and older sister lived with their mother in what is probably the poorest neighborhood in Chicago. It certainly has the highest crime rate. It is an area of old two- and three-story dilapidated wooden tenement buildings on the near West Side, adjacent to the Maxwell Street open-air market place. The concrete sidewalks, like the buildings they border, are slanted, broken, and full of holes. Mrs. Thompson had once worked as a hotel maid, but about the same time James started to get in trouble she had a heart attack, and the family went on public assistance.

Thompson was first brought to the Juvenile Court when he was ten, on a truancy charge. Shortly after, he was brought to court again for being a passenger in a stolen automobile, and a public defender admitted Thompson's guilt for this act. He was placed on probation, and appeared frequently in court throughout the next two years, mostly for truancy. He was sent to a special detention school for truants conducted by the Board of Education, but ran away often—and these acts, too, brought him back into court. Finally, he was committed to the Department of Corrections as a probation violator, spent about a year at St. Charles, and at the time of trial had been at Sheridan for two years.

When Thompson testified, he was sixteen years old—a tall, well-built, fast-talking, swaggering youngster with an almost constant sneer. That, along with his Afro, did not endear him to the rural fellows who worked as guards at Sheridan. It was Thompson's unrebutted testimony that he was kept in solitary confinement for about nine months out of his two years at Sheridan, once for two and a half months at a stretch. His worst ordeal came after he had struck a teacher, when he was kept in solitary for thirty-five days and was given four shots of Thorazine a day for thirty of them.

> Captain Shockley came and got me and took me back to the building. I went to my room and stayed in my room for about fifteen minutes. Then he come right back and took me over there to put me on shots.

I got two shots and come back to my room. I went to sleep for about half an hour. Then they waked me up. They had to carry me over there to get some more shots, because I couldn't walk. When they woke me up I was laying on the floor but I remember getting into bed when I got back from getting my first shots. I remember getting in bed. Then I went to sleep. Then again I woke up to go to the washroom.

When they woke me up to take me back over there, they picked me up off the floor and put my shoes on, put my clothes on.

Q: How many shots did you receive after this scuffle with the teacher?

A: I received four shots that day.

Q: Did you receive any other shots on any other day?

A: I received shots thirty days. I been on shots two times for thirty days.

Q: And were you also placed in solitary confinement as a result of this fight?

A: Thirty-five days.

Our last complaining witness, John Topps, had his seventeenth birthday during the court proceedings. John was a tall, slender youth whose light coloring and Caucasian features belied his Puerto Rican and black background. Although the DOC insisted that his intelligence was below normal, John seemed to us to be a sensitive and bright youngster. His testimony, like his conversation, was given in soft-spoken, well-modulated tones, and his grammar and syntax were those of any well-educated person.

John had grown up on Chicago's West Side in a big family. His stepfather, whom his mother had married when John was very young, was a well-respected Chicago homicide detective who did not get along with the thin, aesthetic boy, and according to psychiatric and social work reports, John had a certain jealousy toward and rivalry with him. The mother and stepfather fought frequently over John and for a time John had been sent to live with his grandparents—which again, according to the social worker who investigated the case, made John feel rejected. In April 1968, during the riots on Chicago's West Side following the death of Martin Luther King, John was arrested along with thousands of other youngsters for arson. The case was dismissed almost immediately, but the charge was to haunt him through his career with the DOC.

Several months later, John was charged with being a runaway and put on probation. Soon he was sent to the DOC for violating the probation by again absenting himself from home without his parents' permission. A psychiatrist had previously recommended family counseling, but none occurred. The judge suggested to the parents that John could get something out of going to one of the DOC forestry camps, and the mother agreed. But, the DOC refused to send him to a forestry camp because of his "arson" background. He was sent instead to St. Charles, where he stayed for about ten months before being released on parole. Two weeks later, he was back with the DOC, this time on his way to Sheridan, because his father had told the parole officer that John was experimenting with drugs.

John had been in Sheridan for two years when he testified. The Sheridan records showed that during his first eleven months there he was kept in solitary for about 180 days. At the time of the hearing, he had been in solitary for seven consecutive months for attacking and seriously injuring a guard. Unlike his three fellow petitioners, John had pretty much avoided the needle at Sheridan, getting shots on only one occasion. During his twenty-five months at Sheridan, John saw a psychiatrist twice, for several minutes.

The last witness for our case was Ronald Clay, also an inmate at Sheridan. Clay had been at Sheridan for almost three and a half years when called to testify. Although he was not a plaintiff, he had been present in January 1971 when Robert Marvin Smith, another Sheridan inmate, had died at the institution. Smith's death had touched off several riots at Sheridan (including, according to Topps, Topps's attack on the guard), for the inmates apparently felt that the administration's use of Thorazine on him had been a contributing factor in his death. Smith, a severe asthmatic, had been in solitary confinement at the time of his death; Clay was also in solitary on upper tier C-7 at the time Smith died and had received Thorazine shots along with him.

With the state objecting to almost every question and the court overruling most of these objections, Clay told the court that he and Smith were given Thorazine while they were in solitary confinement for "ranking" on the doors. He claimed that they were "ranking" because Smith was having an attack and needed "a certain type of medicine which he sprayed in his mouth (according to Clay)." The boys were given two shots of Thorazine a day for five or six days before Smith's death. Clay said that he wrote a letter to the Superintendent about Smith's deteriorating asthmatic condition, but the Superintendent sent word back that the use of drugs on an inmate was a medical decision. When the doctor discovered that Clay had written the letter, he threatened the boys with more Thorazine.

Before a hushed gallery Clay said that he, Smith, and another inmate named Williams were taken to the medical building by Sergeant Watts for their shots on the afternoon before Smith died.

Q: And did you receive a shot of Thorazine?

A: Yes, I did.

Q: And who gave you that shot?

A: The nurse, Miss Beldon.

Q: And did Robert Marvin Smith receive a shot of Thorazine?

MR. FRIEDMAN: Objection—irrelevant.

THE COURT: If you know.

MR. FRIEDMAN: I would object if he does know, if the Court please.

THE COURT: He may answer.

BY THE WITNESS:

A: Ah well, I wasn't there when they was giving it to him, but I was there when they told him to drop his pants, and I assume this is what they was giving him.

MR. FRIEDMAN: I would ask the answer be striken [*sic*], his assumption. The witness has stated he does not know.

THE COURT: Well, why would they tell him to drop his pants?

MR. FRIEDMAN: If the Court please, the statement of the witness is, I assume, that this is what he would be given. I object to the statement and ask that the answer be striken [*sic*].

THE COURT: I will allow the answer to stand and consider it as to the weight to be given to his testimony.

BY MR. MURPHY:

Q: Now, after Robert Marvin Smith dropped his pants, what happened to you?

A: Well, I was told to be handcuffed back up with the other inmate, to be taken back to the building, so more could be brought over for shots.

Q: Now, did Robert Marvin Smith go back to the building with you?

MR. FRIEDMAN: I would object to it—leading.

THE COURT: He may answer.

BY THE WITNESS:

A: No, he didn't go back with us. They kept him over there for a little while longer.

BY MR. MURPHY:

Q: And did you see him again that evening?

A: Yes, I did.

Q: When was the next time you saw him?

A: About five minutes later.

Q: And would you describe whom he was with and what his condition was when you saw him?

MR. FRIEDMAN: Objection—irrelevant, Your Honor.

THE COURT: He may answer.

BY THE WITNESS:

A: Well, he was handcuffed. They were taking the handcuffs off of him, putting him back in his room. He was breathing real hard. I asked him did they give him shots. He said yes, they gave him tranquilizer shots. They put him back in his cell and shut the door and walked away. . . .

BY MR. MURPHY:

Q: Will you continue with your response?

A: As I said, the shots were overcoming me. I had to go to bed. They were making me drowsy.

MR. FRIEDMAN: I move the answer be striken.

THE COURT: Denied. Go ahead.

BY MR. MURPHY:

Q: Did you fall asleep then?

A: Well, not right off, About five, ten minutes later I went off to sleep.

Q: Did you later wake up that night?

A: Yes. I heard a lot of noise which woke me up.

Q: And what was that noise? Were you able to determine?

A: It was the sounds of a lot of oxygen, oxygen tanks and such things.

Q: And were they in Smith's room?

A: They were right across the hall from me. They were in his room. Quite a few people had oxygen on him.

Smith was dead within five minutes. The autopsy gave the causes of death as "acute cardio-respiratory failure due to *status asthmaticus,* severe. Pulmonary emphysema. Right heart enlargement."

The pharmaceutical company that produces Thorazine points out, "Thorazine cannot substitute for other psychiatric techniques, adequate facilities, and dedicated knowledgeable personnel." In the literature accompanying the drug, the company warns that "Thorazine should be used with caution on patients with chronic respiratory disorders such as severe asthma, emphysema and acute respiratory infection. This is particularly true when administering the drug to children. Because Thorazine can suppress the cough reflex, aspiration of vomitus is possible."

5

Care, Custody, and Maximum Security: Our Battle in the Federal Courts

BY THE TIME we finished our case, the burden of proof switched to the state, which had three theoretical avenues open to it. The attorneys could try to disprove the boys' stories; they could try to demonstrate that what was happening at Sheridan was done as part of a legitimate therapy and treatment program which the boys were not sophisticated enough to understand; or they could admit that abuses had occurred and promise to improve the situation. But the first alternative was not open to the state, because we had the Department of Corrections records which substantiated the boys' testimony. The third avenue never occurred to them. So the state had to rationalize the punishment as treatment. To do this, the state relied primarily on four witnesses: David Brierton, the new Superintendent at Sheridan; Dr. Marvin Ziporin, a psychiatrist who worked for the DOC at their medium-security institutions; George Beto, Director of the Texas DOC; and Sanger Powers, his counterpart in Wisconsin.

The first and best witness for the state was David Brierton. Brierton testified that he had released about 100 boys from Sheridan since he had become Superintendent five weeks before. He had instituted other reforms—broadening letter-writing privileges to allow the boys to write to others than members of their family, liberalizing commissary privileges to include soaps, mouthwashes, Noxzema, and other items for the large black population, such as soaps and aids for their hair and complexion. He testified that he was planning to make isolation, segregation, and solitary confinement more palatable. Thorazine had been used, to Brierton's knowledge, only once during the time he had been at Sheridan, and he had instructed his staff that, although the administration of drugs was a medical decision, it should not be used for punishment or simply to control behavior.

The next two witnesses were George Beto and Sanger Powers. These witnesses gave various justifications for maximum-security penal institutions for children, although neither had ever actually run one of them. On cross-examination, Beto stated his belief that if a boy were to curse at a guard and use racial epithets, this would be a good enough reason to keep him in solitary confinement. He further thought that as long as a boy continued to "rank," scream, and yell while in solitary confinement, it was "highly possible" that he would keep the boy on in solitary, even if such conduct lasted for as long as seventeen consecutive months—and even if the boy had been put there for unjustifiable reasons in the first place.

The major portion of Beto's very brief testimony was that maximum-security institutions for youths were needed for ". . . the protection of the individual, the protection of the individual offender, the protection of his peers and the maintenance of order, tranquillity, within the institution. It is difficult to carry on any type of rehabilitative program unless there is discipline and order within the institution." He would not characterize Sheridan as a prison, he said, but as a "youthful-offender facility." On cross-examination, he volunteered that of all the prisons he had visited in Illinois, Sheridan seemed the least prisonlike—although he could not measure how much less.

THE COURT: But it [Sheridan] had cells?

THE WITNESS: Yes, sir.

THE COURT: With bars?

THE WITNESS: Yes, sir.

THE COURT: Cell blocks?

THE WITNESS: Yes sir.

THE COURT: And an administration house on the outside of the gate?

THE WITNESS: (Nodding head.)

BY MR. MURPHY:

Q: You testified you used Thorazine in your adult institutions in Texas, is that correct?

A: Yes, sir.

Q: And you testified that you used solitary confinement or administrative—whatever you called this—

A: "Segregation."

Q: (Continuing)—in your adult institutions in Texas, is that correct?

A: Yes, sir.

Q: And you testified you had cells in your adult institutions in Texas, is that correct?

A: Yes, sir.

Q: I assume in some of your adult institutions you have walls around the institution, is that correct, or fences?

A: Yes. Oddly enough, the one of the fourteen institutions which is the secondmost [*sic*] relaxed has walls.

Q: And some of your institutions may not have walls or fences around them, is that correct?

A: All but one have either walls or fences.

Q: But you have one adult institution for adult criminals with no fence or wall around it, is that right?

A: Yes.

Q: And, I assume, in most of your adult institutions you have programs for the adult inmates, is that correct?

A: Yes, sir.

Q: You have schools for them?

A: Yes, sir.

Q: You have vocational programs for them, is that correct?

A: Yes.

Q: Now, assuming that Sheridan—

A: We also have work for them.

Q: You have work for them. Now, assuming that Sheridan had walls around the institution, they have cells, they have solitary confinement, they have administrative segregation, they have Thorazine and they have a few programs for the children, would you tell us how in fact your adult jails or prisons, as you describe them, differ from Sheridan.

MR. FRIEDMAN: Object, if the Court please. It is the ultimate issue of law for this Court to determine.

THE COURT: Do you mean I am to determine whether or not Texas provides for its adults better than Illinois does for its juveniles? No, that is not the ultimate question. But he may answer.

BY THE WITNESS:

A: I think you oversimplified the difference, Counsel.

BY MR. MURPHY:

Q: What is the difference aside from age?

A: I think you fail to realize that, very frequently, juveniles are more sophisticated in their criminality than older offenders and, secondly, there is less of a sense of responsibility regarding the consequences of their actions.

For instance, of the fourteen institutions which I operate, for which I am responsible, I would rather be warden of our security [unit]—the Alcatraz of the system, the Ellis unit, where we have 1500 multiple recidivists, high escape risks, agitators—I would much rather be the warden of that unit, where we have boys between the ages of sixteen and twenty-one. I would sleep better at night.

In 1961, George Beto had been the chairman of a state commission which had prepared a report on Illinois prisons. Also on this same commission was Sanger Powers, now Director of the Wisconsin DOC, and the man who followed Beto to the witness stand. The state's theory in putting Powers and Beto on the stand was apparently to show, through their expertise, that Sheridan was not similar to an adult penal institution.

Winston Moore, Director of the Cook County DOC, had told us about the 1961 prison report and helped us to get a copy, and we were able to use it, ironically enough, to discredit much of Beto's and Powers' testimonies. The report had characterized Sheridan as a prisonlike security institution, with barred windows and steel doors. The witnesses were forced to admit on cross-examination that they had not been to Sheridan since 1961, and at that time had subscribed to the portion of the report which read: "The boys at the industrial school are being detained in a security cellblock institution which has relied primarily on security of custody and has very little in the way of an educational or treatment program. The boys are undergoing an experience resembling that given the adult criminal confined in prison."

There were other problems and other contradictions which the state's witnesses had to cope with. During the earlier Sheridan trial, before Judge White, and after the boys had testified about the punishments they received at Sheridan, there had been what appeared to be retaliatory actions taken against them. The water in C-7, the isolation unit, had been shut off for several days, and the boys on that tier block had their clothes and bedclothes taken from them. Larry Woodson testified before Judge Parsons about all of this, and he went on to explain that at times men from the towns surrounding Sheridan helped the guards in the monthly cell searches.

Although the state did not attempt to rebut the boys' central allegations, they did try to rebut this portion of their testimony. Guard Ronald Reed was put on the stand to testify that he could not recall seeing other than Sheridan employees or state police participate in these searches. But on cross-examination, Reed admitted that both counselors and guards were used to search the cells, and he described them and the tier blocks in Sheridan in detail.

The state then called Ed Powell, an administrative assistant to Judge White. Powell testified that, at Judge White's direction, he went to Sheridan to question the boys concerning their allegations of retaliatory punishment. When he questioned them, he said, none of them complained about any punishments taken against them because of their testimony.

Now it was understandable to us that the state put Powers and Beto on the stand not knowing that we had a copy of their 1961 report, which could undermine the credibility of their testimony about Sheridan. But it was inconceivable to us that they would put Powell on the stand, knowing as they did that we ourselves had questioned Powell after his return from Sheridan. Nevertheless, they did, and we naturally cross-examined him about what the boys told Powell had happened after their testimony before Judge White:

BY MR. MURPHY:

Q: Mr. Powell, how long have you been administrative assistant to Judge White?

A: Since April of this year.

Q: Now, would you classify the fact that Woodson told you —Strike that. Wouldn't you characterize Woodson's statement that he had not had water in his room for four days as a complaint?

MR. FRIEDMAN: Objection to the characterization.

THE COURT: He may answer.

MR. FRIEDMAN: The witness has testified he made no complaints other than the fact that the water had been turned off, and his question of classification calls for a conclusion.

THE COURT: He may answer.

BY THE WITNESS:

A: Other than stating that the water was turned off, he made no other complaints.

BY MR. MURPHY:

Q: So you do characterize that as a complaint?

A: I would assume—

MR. FRIEDMAN: Objection.

THE COURT: Overruled. He may answer.

BY MR. MURPHY:

Q: Did you make any—

THE COURT: I don't hear the answer.

MR. MURPHY: He said that he did classify—

THE WITNESS: I am sorry. I did say yes.

BY MR. MURPHY:

Q: Now, do you recall Larry Woodson telling you that he had no linen in his room?

A: Yes.

Q: Would you classify that as a complaint?

A: Yes.

Q: And do you remember Larry Woodson telling you that his pants were taken away from him, and he was not allowed pants until one hour before his mother came to visit him?

A: Yes.

Q: And would you classify that as a complaint?

A: Yes.

Q: Do you recall Larry Woodson telling you he was placed in solitary confinement upon his return?

A: No, I don't.

Q: And, in fact, were you able to determine whether Larry Woodson was placed in solitary confinement?

A: I could not determine it.

Q: Did you make any effort?

A: Well, the setting was one where we were in the conference room and we did not go to the areas where they were supposed to be confined.

Q: And the conference room was in the administration building?

A: In the administration building.

Q: That is outside the walls, is that correct?

A: Yes, sir.

Q: Now, isn't it a fact that Mr. Goldsher is the legal advisor to the Department of Corrections?

A: Yes, sir.

Q: And he was in the room at the time you interviewed the boy, is that not correct?

A: Yes.

Q: And there were three guards in the room also?

A: Yes.

Q: And there was a Mr. Osbourne, also an adviser to the Department of Corrections, is that correct?

A: I don't know the name of the other gentleman. I can't recall it offhand. But there was another person.

Q: And Mr. Woodson was in handcuffs at the time, is that correct?

A: That is right.

Q: Now, did Judge White at any time make any statement to you after your return as to whether you should have spoken to the boys by themselves?

MR. FRIEDMAN: Objection.

THE COURT: Overruled. He may answer.

BY THE WITNESS:

A: He asked me why we did not speak to them by themselves, and we told him at that time we had asked could it be done and we were denied the privilege.

MR. MURPHY: I see. Thank you very much.

THE COURT: Is there any redirect?

MR. FRIEDMAN: No, Your Honor.

The state's last witness was Marvin Ziporin, a psychiatrist who worked at the Department of Corrections' medium-security institutions. At the hearing before Judge White, the state had called two other psychiatrists, Dr. Aldo Cahue, the part-time psychiatrist at Sheridan, and Dr. Kermit Mehlinger, a psychiatrist at Cook County Hospital, both of whom had ended up by harming the state's case. Dr. Cahue had disagreed with both Superintendent Rowe and Dr. Smith that Earl Lasser's 262 days of solitary confinement was "milieu therapy," and had acknowledged that such confinement could cause a personality breakdown which might have led to Lasser's continued bad behavior and to his attempted suicide. He had nothing to do with the administration of Thorazine and was not consulted about the effects of Thorazine or solitary confinement. Dr. Mehlinger was no less candid. So we knew that the state would call neither Dr. Cahue nor Dr. Mehlinger to testify in the federal hearing. But Dr. Ziporin's testimony on direct examination was convincing. The therapy at Sheridan, he said, was basically "negative reinforcement." When an inmate acted in an undesirable and antisocial manner, placing him in solitary confinement removed him from the stress situation and also informed the boy that his behavior would not be tolerated. One could also remove the boy from the stress by intervening with chemical therapy—Thorazine— and this aided in illustrating "to the patient that his behavior is self-destructive."

Psychiatrists are very difficult witnesses to cross-examine because, like witch doctors and theologians, they set themselves up within a realm of knowledge that seems supernatural. One rudimentary technique employed in cross-examining a witness of this type is to ask a series of questions which, to the witness, seem reasonable and to which he must take a position favorable to his client, but which ultimately nudge him, inch by inch, out on a limb, until the ultimate series of questions make him look ridiculous to the tryer of fact.

After several cross-examining questions concerning Thorazine and solitary confinement, we asked Dr. Ziporin what the effect of 262 days of solitary confinement might have been in Earl Lasser's initial fifteen months at Sheridan. Dr. Ziporin replied that there were several possible consequences: 1) the child could be completely unaffected, 2) it might "stimulate creative imagination," 3) it might effect "a salutary response in terms of future behavioral patterns," or 4) it could have "a detrimental effect, stimulating anxiety." When pressed to give examples of people who had spent protracted periods in solitary confinement and who had experienced creative side effects, Dr. Ziporin mentioned Cervantes and some revolutionary leaders in Russia who had been exiled to Siberia.

Dr. Ziporin agreed that the effects of 100 miligrams of Thorazine would last about four hours. One question which had been unresolved both before Judge White and Judge Parsons, was why a doctor would prescribe 100 miligrams twice a day for four consecutive days when the drug was purportedly given to calm a boy down. Assumedly, if the effects wore off in four hours, the boy would again be threatening four hours after the effects of the shot wore off and before he received a second dose. If he were not threatening, and from the testimony, most appeared not to be, then the question was, why continue the shots if not for punishment purposes? Dr. Ziporin claimed that a doctor might not want to keep up a steady level of shots at full capacity because of the side effects. We then asked why it would be necessary to give James Thompson four shots a day of Thorazine for thirty consecutive days. Dr. Ziporin did a complete turnabout and replied that the answer was clear. "It was given in an attempt to exercise a therapeutic response on the patient and to improve his general psychiatric status." From the circumstances in the case, he said, it was obvious that there was planning involved in this drug treatment, and one would have to assume that the effect was therapeutic rather than punitive. "This is the kind of approach you use in a total therapeutic program."

Later, Dr. Marvin Schwarz, director of the departments of psychiatry at several Chicago hospitals as well as a professor of psychiatry, said of the same case: "I could see where it would have superb punitive purposes if this were the intent; it would indicate to the boy that the punishment for talking in school was certainly very high, but I don't see it as having therapeutic purposes from the standpoint of assisting that boy to understand the nature of his conflict, developing appropriate impulse control, ultimate growth and development, and rehabilitation into the community." And when Dr. Schwarz was told about Earl Lasser and his 262 days in solitary, his description of the probable effects, instead of resorting to the almost 400-year-old and not exactly comparable case of Cervantes, was blunt and to the point: "Extreme regression, with destruction in many areas of ego strength, with some questions as to how reversible some of these effects might be, but certainly no opportunity for any meaningful growth and development."

We called Dr. Schwarz to the stand later in the hearing specifically to counter Dr. Ziporin's testimony. Dr. Schwarz was a brilliant and generous man—he had published many books, articles, and a textbook in psychiatry, and had once taught statistics and nuclear physics as well—who donated his services to our office in this and other cases free of charge. His private clientele was mostly made up of wealthy teen-agers from North Shore suburbs, and he was later to testify that the state was imprisoning poor children for the same acts for which wealthy children came to him or were put in the best private psychiatric clinics.

Dr. Schwarz testified that Thorazine was "an excellent drug as part of a total treatment program" but that it made no sense in absence of such a psychiatric program. The drug has considerable side effects, he pointed out, and can cause cardiovascular attacks in asthmatics, jaundice, and, in rare instances, a fatal affliction in which white blood cells cease reproduction. The intramuscular injections are very painful and, in instances of repeated long-term injections for punitive purposes, could cause extreme hostility.

He went on to identify the paradox which he considered characteristic of Sheridan and similar institutions: "The kid is put in the cell, he is shot up with Thorazine, he is locked in solitary, and we say this is not punishment, this is a rehabilitative program. Now, I don't know if it is confusing to children; it is very confusing to me, and I have certainly never understood this." It might be better, Dr. Schwarz argued, to acknowledge that a place like Sheridan *was* punitive, and work from there. On the issue of indeterminate sentencing, which lay at the very center of our case, Dr. Schwarz said:

> If our institution, in reality, is not rehabilitative but punitive, then we must define it as punitive, and correlate the punishment with what they are punishing him for.
>
> If it is a jail, we must tie things into the sentences for the jail, and in our culture this is tied into the nature of the crime. Namely, if we are putting people into penal institutions as a punitive device, then the child expects some correlation between the punishment he receives and what he did.

But Dr. Schwarz admitted that there were no easy answers:

> I think it is clear that we must begin to develop new techniques. . . .
>
> The difficulty we run into is that the ghetto has so much stress and has so many elements which are destructive to adolescents to begin with, that it is very difficult to talk about the development of alternative solutions. But it is quite clear that the existing solutions in terms of institutions such as Sheri-

> dan do not represent a satisfactory solution—not to the problems of the Department of Corrections, but to the problems of our society. . . .
>
> The dilemma that we have is that professional groups, both within society and within the correctional field, have devoted remarkably little of our funds and efforts to this question compared to the funds we are spending on the operation of such institutions.

The state had rested its case after calling Dr. Ziporin, and aside from rebutting Dr. Ziporin's testimony with Dr. Schwarz, we really had no need to do anything else. We had not only the unrebutted testimony of the four boys and Ronald Clay but the damaging admissions made by the state's witnesses on cross-examination. Still, we felt it was important to establish accountability for the actions at Sheridan, so we subpoenaed Peter Bensinger, Director of the Illinois Department of Corrections, and Joseph Coughlin, his assistant in charge of the Juvenile Division. And, before calling them, we brought Sheridan's Chief of Security and Captain of the Guards to the stand.

Nicholas Mellas, Chief of Security, had been dismissed from Sheridan in 1961 but rehired after a Civil Service Commission hearing. Everett Shockley, the chief guard, had worked at the Illinois State Penitentiary before coming to Sheridan in 1961. Both were big, burly men in their forties, and both attempted to evade our questions.

Mellas agreed that it was conceivable that a boy could have been in solitary for three or four consecutive months in his experience, and though he did not keep track of the longest time a boy was on Thorazine, he did think it was possible that boys had been on for as much as twenty consecutive days. At first, he said that Sheridan had more recreational facilities than the Illinois State Penitentiary, but when pressed as to what these were, he replied that he wasn't sure.

When we asked Shockley what was the longest he remembered a boy being in solitary confinement, he said he would hate to guess, but that he could remember cases of a week or maybe two. However, when pressed on the case of a boy who had been in solitary between May and December 1970, he recalled the incident but said that the boy had refused to come out of the cell! Was it possible that boys had been in solitary for up to four months, we asked, and Shockley agreed that this was possible.

We then asked Shockley if he had ever stated that younger boys should be put together with the older ones so that the latter could work out their sexual aggressions. Shockley denied this, and the two State's Attorneys insisted that we prove this alleged statement. We never did, because the man who told us about it was Winston Moore, the much-respected Director of Cook County Corrections. (I asked Moore to testify concerning Shockley's statement, and at first he agreed, but later said he couldn't. About a year later, he told me that Bensinger had told his superior, Cook County Sheriff Richard Elrod, that if Moore testified, federal funds would be cut off to the Cook County penal system. Under the circumstances, I did not blame Moore for not testifying.)

The State's Attorneys had objected when we subpoenaed Coughlin and Bensinger, and this seemed to the outside observer a very odd position to take. After all, they had called the directors of the Wisconsin and Texas DOCs to the stand; how could they deny that we had good precedents to call Illinois' own Director of Corrections? Judge Parsons overruled their objections.

Coughlin, a stylishly dressed, fifty-year-old social worker, was just the sort of witness we had anticipated. The administration of Thorazine was a medical decision to be made by medical doctors, he said, and he had to trust their judgment. Indeed, if his own son were pumped full of Thorazine, as the boys at Sheridan had been, he would have no objections. Solitary confinement was necessary because it helped to establish manly characters.

Coughlin's remarks were brief, and he did not try to evade our questions. We did not have such luck with Bensinger.

There were really only two basic questions we wanted Bensinger to answer: what was the DOCs policy on indeterminate sentencing? And what was his opinion as to solitary confinement and Thorazine? Bensinger was on the stand for two full days, and the state never attempted to cross-examine him at all. His answers to our own direct examination were evasive, and the state objected to almost every one of our questions. Those were two *long* days. Of course, the issue of indeterminate sentencing was the crux of our lawsuit. The theory behind indeterminate sentencing was to keep a boy in custody until he was rehabilitated. If he became a behavioral problem or refused to cooperate with authorities, he would, *regardless of the nature of his crime,* not only be incarcerated for a very long time but also be sent to progressively more punitive institutions. This paradox was brought home most pointedly in the case of John Topps, who was convicted of merely running away from home but who spent almost a year at St. Charles and two years in Sheridan.

Bensinger's background was Brahmin to say the least. Coming from inherited wealth, he had graduated from Phillips Exeter and Yale University. His ruddy, cherubic face made him look younger than his thirty-seven or thirty-eight years, and he had a carefully cultivated reputation as one of the state's leading Republican liberals.

Bensinger testified that the Parole and Pardon Board had at his urging adopted a rule giving annual parole consideration for each juvenile inmate in Illinois. Though the rule may have been in effect, the officials at Sheridan were not following it, and none of our clients had ever had a parole consideration. We asked him whether he knew if the rule was in effect prior to September 1971, before we filed the lawsuit. For an entire morning and most of an afternoon, he evaded this simple question, sometimes answering one way, sometimes the other, but mostly giving speeches.

Finally, he said that inmates are considered for parole "as soon as it is deemed in the best interest of each individual committed to our care and the best interest of our community." Judge Parsons then reasoned that Bensinger's testimony meant that the annual review program had not been in effect at Sheridan prior to September, to which the state objected. Judge Parsons then struck the question and answer that had led to this inference and instructed us to rephrase the question. For another hour, we tried to get Bensinger to answer the question; finally, he stated that Coughlin had told him that the annual review policy was in effect prior to September 1971.

We then showed Bensinger three rules of the DOC, one of which had been in existence for many months and two of which had gone into effect the summer before. Each of these declared that an inmate at Sheridan would be ineligible for parole until he had completed an assigned program or, if he were on a "set," until he was off the "set." Bensinger insisted that the annual parole review would be in effect anyway, but when we asked him how the Board could review the case of a boy at Sheridan if the officials at the institution did not give the boy's file or name to it, Bensinger said he had no knowledge of the process by which the reviews took place. He advised that we contact the Director of the Parole Board and gave us his phone number and address.

We moved on to Thorazine. Bensinger said that this was a medical matter and beyond his expertise. He was questioned on the amount of solitary confinement and Thorazine given Earl Lasser. What specifically, did he think of Earl's being in solitary between December 28, 1969, and March 12, 1970? In general, Bensinger responded, it was up to the DOC to provide treatment, motivation, and discipline for the individual; it was also their responsibility to protect others whom the individual might harm. Although Bensinger never did answer the question whether the continued confinement might itself have caused the behavior that led to more confinement, he agreed that in Lasser's case there were desirable alternatives to solitary confinement, although, he said, the population of the institution at that time did not allow it.

Lasser had once been put in solitary for "talking in class," and we asked Bensinger whether this at least might not be a case of overkill. He replied that Lasser, after all, could have been disrupting the class. So we asked Bensinger whether *he* had ever received such a punishment for a similar offense when he was in school. He more or less denied that he ever talked out of turn in class. "At the time, I was at the Phillips Exeter Academy in New Hampshire, Mr. Murphy, and it has been twenty years, I can't recall that I was, at that time, remonstrated by a teacher." Still, he could not recall that any other boy had been placed in solitary confinement at Exeter for a similar offense.

Bensinger made a dull witness, with his stubborn evasiveness and his ignorance of what was going on at Sheridan. But on the morning of his second day of testimony, something lively happened, and it perfectly expressed the paranoia that afflicts prison and correctional bureaucrats. A woman who supervised what seemed to be a good program for juvenile parolees at the DOC brought some Sheridan parolees to the court to watch the hearing, apparently at Judge Parsons' suggestion. They were milling about in the hall before the session began, and I talked to some of them about Robert Smith's death, since several had been in the cellblock at that time and were willing to testify about it. Then I had to go back into the courtroom to speak to Lew, and when I returned, the woman was talking to them. I could make out only a little bit of what she was saying, but right afterward one of the boys came to me and said that he could not testify because the woman had told them their paroles could be revoked if they testified. I confronted the woman immediately and asked her if this were true. It was conceivable, she said, that their paroles could be revoked. Then she turned her back and walked into the courtroom. I followed her and tried to talk some more with her, but she refused. I asked her her name and for whom she worked, and again she refused to answer. I gave up, and went to counsel table. Bensinger, who was sitting in the courtroom, went up to her, whispered something, and together they quickly left the courtroom. Naturally, I followed and watched them talking down the hall. I went back into the court, and about five minutes later the two returned. Almost immediately, and before the trial resumed, the woman and the boys departed.

As soon as Bensinger took the stand, I asked him if the woman dressed in red and previously sitting in the third row were employed by the Department of Corrections, and he replied that he thought that she was. Bensinger denied knowing anything about the woman telling the boys their paroles would be revoked if they testified, but he admitted that he had a conversation with her—it had nothing to do with the boys' testimony, he said. When I tried to ask him what the conversation was about, the Assistant Attorney General objected and Judge Parsons sustained the objection. When I asked Bensinger if he would mind the boys' testifying, he stated, "I would have an interest as Director of Corrections and would want to consult with the legal custodian, their counselors, as to what the implications for their own personal programs would be."

We subpoenaed the lady in the red dress. To our amazement, she swore under oath that she had never had a conversation with me in the hallway and did not recall having a conversation with Bensinger—thus contradicting not only me but Bensinger himself. She went on to claim that she never told the boys their paroles would be revoked and did not know why they refused to testify. Later, I took the stand myself to rebut her testimony about our little chat.

As the hearing dragged on through October and November, it became clearer and clearer that Judge Parsons would rule in our favor, for he was obviously shocked and disgusted by what he heard. The only question was just how broad his ultimate order would be. The state had not attempted to disprove our accusations and only the testimony of Dr. Ziporin, whose credibility was severely undermined on cross-examination, attempted to claim that what happened at Sheridan was "rehabilitation and treatment." By the end of the hearing, reports on it were being featured and headlined in all the daily newspapers, and public reaction was compelling the DOC to parole several boys each week from the institution.

Toward the end of the trial, we had to recall Larry Woodson to clarify certain matters in his testimony.

In many ways, Larry was the easiest of our four boys to like. John Topps was the most intelligent and also the most sympathetic, for his trouble with the authorities was so clearly not his fault—he had never been convicted of a criminal offense. But Larry's testimony was very appealing—he was loud and brash, but he was strikingly sincere and truthful. He admitted that he had caused many disturbances for which he thought he was justifiably placed in solitary. But there were many other things for which he was placed in solitary that he could not understand. Anyway, we called Larry back to the stand toward the end of our rebuttal to testify about how the boys at Sheridan had been treated after they testified at the first hearing before Judge White. We questioned him, the state cross-examined him, and then, as Larry was about to leave the stand, Judge Parsons engaged him in conversation:

> THE COURT: I notice you don't stand straight. What is the matter? Can you tell me what is the matter?
>
> THE WITNESS: My mother, she told me I didn't walk like this when I was out. When I was on shots, my buttocks used to get so swollen that the nurse had to shoot me right in the side. You know, they would shoot me over there. I don't know what happened, I just started walking with a limp. She shot me up in the hip, way up by my side.
>
> THE COURT: Can you run and play?

THE WITNESS: I can run and play, but I just have this walk—my mother asked me yesterday could I move around and I told her I could move around pretty fast.

THE COURT: You hold your hand sort of like your fingers are stiff. Why do you do that?

THE WITNESS: My mother told me that I haven't been acting right since I—in the last past five months. I don't know why.

THE COURT: Now, don't be embarrassed by this question: you sound to me like you are a very angry young man when you talk, the way you talk. Is this the way you talk all the time?

THE WITNESS: Yes, sir. They even told me, Topps and Thompson even tell me, everybody tells me this—

THE COURT: That you talk sort of harsh all the time?

THE WITNESS: Yes, harsh.

THE COURT: Do you mean to?

THE WITNESS: No, sir. When I am in my room, that is the only time. Right now I haven't said nothing, over forty words, to nobody within about three weeks. I am trying to stay out of trouble. I hardly say nothing to the guards or nothing.

I say a few words to my brother. He sees me now and then. Me and him get into arguments. I don't hardly say nothing to nobody.

THE COURT: Did you get in arguments before when you were a little boy, before you went into St. Charles?

THE WITNESS: I didn't never get in no arguments, never. I never got in no arguments when I was there.

THE COURT: Did you get along with your mother all right?

THE WITNESS: I get along. She comes out there every Sunday.

THE COURT: How about your father?

THE WITNESS: Yes, he comes out there.

THE COURT: And your grandmother?

THE WITNESS: All of them come out there, my auntie and my sister; she brings—my auntie brings her baby, and my sister and my little brother, they all come out there every week.

THE COURT: Do you want to go home?

THE WITNESS: Yes, sir, I want to go home. Everyone wants to go home. They ain't never allowed it.

THE COURT: Are you tired?

THE WITNESS: I've been tired for the longest.

6

The Demise of Maximum Security

AFTER final argument on November 22, 1971, Judge Parsons issued his oral opinion on the Sheridan case.

This is one of the most difficult matters I have had to try as a Federal Judge. The difficulty has grown from a serious desire on the part of the respondent or his counsel, if not the respondent, to prevent the case from being overheard by the public or spread on the records of this Court. Tactics employed reached close to those traditionally considered reprehensible. . . .

The most humane program established some seventy years ago this year by the State of Illinois, finds itself incorporated in the Juvenile Court Act. It was an effort to adopt what was thought to be a humane program with relation to problem children, children who were disturbed, children who were deserted, children who were mentally or emotionally unbalanced, and just plain difficult children, or a child who was unwilling to conform to structures of society set up by an adult world.

The sponsorship of this was sophisticated social welfare beneficiaries and benefactors and its legislation was the first of any state in the country to be enacted and was then called the first

Juvenile Delinquency Law in the history of the United States. It is known today as the Juvenile Court Act.

Illinois was followed in this program by a vast majority of the rest of the States in the Union. Its philosophy was that children whose parents cannot or would not provide them the proper parental care and guidance and who became destitute or deserted or orphaned or antisocial or unlawful in their conduct, or dangerous to themselves or to the public, could be given a new parent-child relationship. The parent would thus become the State of Illinois, as indeed the father of an illegitimate child in the State of Illinois is the State of Illinois.

This new parent would furnish the child with the excellent type of parenthood which its real parent should have furnished but didn't. That parenthood should continue throughout the then childhood of the infant until, if necessary, the infant was twenty-one years old, whereupon it would become an adult and thus responsible for itself.

If they commit crimes but merely found to be juvenile delinquents and made wards of the State. So also if their conduct did not comport with social standards of good conduct, they judicially should be declared wards of the State, the State of Illinois thus becoming their parent, and a special court called into session to so declare it would set up to institute and guide a program for the care of the infant. This concept, refined exists today and it has existed over a number of years.

Thus, a runaway child or one who would not go to school, or one who would steal from a store a garment worth less than $50, or one who would be found riding in a car that had been stolen, would not be convicted of a crime but would be declared a juvenile delinquent and, thus, placed into the parenthood of the State of Illinois for a period of up to his twenty-first birthday. Even today State parenthood can continue until that twenty-first birthday, despite the fact that we have reduced the age of voting down to eighteen years.

For a boy, by the time the court has moved with relation to his welfare, may himself have changed, have grown, have become a man, but may still be a ward of the State of Illinois.

A byproduct of this rather sanctified adult condescension has included among other things court proceedings of a different type to that which adults are themselves exposed. . . .

It is a recognized principle of law that rights guaranteed by the Constitution and laws of the United States inure as much to the protection of the newborn infant as indeed they do to the most venerable adult or citizen among us.

When you read of the ages of these fifty-five men who wrote the Consititution of the United States, and of the fact that among the signers of that Constitution were persons too young to hold any of the offices that had been created by them in that Constitution, and the fact that in over seventy years of Illinois leadership, the states of our nation have until now retained a sort of second-class citizenship for its children, one wonders where the real meaning of the Constitution has found its way into the language of us adults who administer the Code of the State of Illinois. . . .

The evidence in conclusion is that Sheridan is a penitentiary-type institution. I use the word "penitentiary" advisedly, for a penitentiary-type institution is one that has its foundations in the history of those prisons into which persons were placed in cells that were like dungeons, under the idea that by so being placed, they could contemplate upon their sins, they could ask forgiveness and be absolved, and possibly be released and they could cheer themselves.

That is the hallmark of a penitentiary-type institution, as in the instances of all of the boys, no adult could ever be required to spend the same amount of time in a penitentiary-type institution for the same conduct of which these four petitioners before me have been required to spend. No adult could be required to spend half the time that any one of these boys has spent in a penitentiary-type institution for conduct equivalent to that for which they were sentenced.

This constitutes, as a matter of fact and as a matter of law, blatant and irrefutably the creation as to them of a classification not justified at law, which constitutes a violation of the equal protection of the laws clause of the Fourteenth Amendment to the Constitution of the United States.

I am quick to acknowledge that this is not a class action, but, nevertheless, they are representative of a discriminatory type of classification. Because of their age they have been discriminated against, a clear violation not only of the law of the State of Illinois but, indeed, of the Fourteenth Amendment to the Constitution of the United States.

This alone would be sufficient to justify my granting their petitions. But this is not all. The State system has not been a benevolent one, as it was intended to be by the statute; else how could it in its benevolence utilize Thorazine for purposes of punishment of a child, for purposes of control and punishment?

The language, and I quote, which is sent out by the owner and manufacturer—the owner of the patent and manufacturer of this drug, Thorazine, in what is called the "Dear Doctor" card to all physicians throughout the United States and all pharmaceutical houses and pharmacists throughout the United States, is as follows, and I quote:

> "Chlorpronazine [that is the chemical word for Thorazine] has been available to American physicians since 1954. The drug has exerted a profound influence on medicine in general and in the treatment of mental illness in particular. Since 1954 it has been more thoroughly investigated, more extensively documented and more widely used than any other agent of its kind.
>
> "Its principal use is in the treatment of severe mental and

emotional disorders. It is a potent tranquilizer and is available only through a physician's prescription. As with all prescription drugs, chlorpronazine should only be administered by or under the supervision of a qualified physician.

"Chlorpronazine should be administered cautiously to persons with suspected heart disease. Because of its central nervous system depressant effect, the drug product should be used with caution in patients with chronic respiratory disorders, such as severe asthma, emphysema and acute respiratory infections, particularly in children.

"The use of chlorpronazine in any non-medical situation is improper and constitutes a serious form of drug abuse."

This is word for word from the literature furnished with the drug to the medical profession and pharmacists in accordance with the requirements of the Pure Food and Drug Administration of the United States. This also comports with the testimony of the last witness for respondent—rather, for petitioners—the psychiatrist, who stated that it was not indicated in any way in use with relation to the petitioners before me. Yet its use with relation to that of abuse, that of punishment, that for which the witness said if he found the parents of the children using, he would give the information to the State's Attorney to have them prosecuted under child abuse laws.

In fairness to the pharmaceutical company which owns this patent, I have read this statement. The pharmaceutical company does not approve its use in any prison throughout the United States except in support of psychotherapy.

Though it would be obiter dicta, I would be derelict if I were not to protect the pharmaceutical house from any abusive concept that would result from my reading this.

As for solitary confinement, there was not a witness before me who did not admit that it has no therapeutic effect beyond a period . . . in excess of twenty-four hours.

If I have learned anything from this case, I have learned that as to all prisons throughout the United States neither Thorazine nor solitary confinement are procedures of a rehabilitative nature. If there is any warning that I might give, it is a warning of this pharmaceutical company that this drug is not to be used for control of prisoners. It is a warning of the psychiatrist who testified before me that solitary confinement is not rehabilitative.

Gentlemen, I conclude it is my order and I do clearly so order as follows—and any order, of course, that I give is subject to appeal. I respect the higher court.

First, that the petitioners herein who remain at Sheridan shall within twenty-four hours of this date, 12 Noon today, be released from custody at Sheridan.

Second, that the custody into which they are released be such as will provide a parent-child relationship, as I stated as is contemplated by the statute itself, and if not in a home, in an institution that provides that type of relationship.

Third, that as to these petitioners, wherever they may be in custody, that they not be submitted to solitary confinement and that they not be submitted to the use of Thorazine or any other tranquilizer whatsoever for purposes of mere control, and certainly that they not be submitted to the use of Thorazine or any other tranquilizer for purposes of punishment, and I direct that the United States Marshal by 4 p.m. tomorrow report to me that these boys who remain in such custody be transferred, and in case he reports that they have not been so transferred, that the United States Marshal stand by for further orders of this Court.

EACH OF our four boys was released to his family except John Topps, who was awaiting trial in LaSalle County on a felony charge of aggravated battery. Two months later, after a conference with the State's Attorney's office in that small, rural county, we pleaded John guilty to a misdemeanor of simple battery and he was sentenced to "not less than one or more than two years" in the Illinois State Penitentiary. The nine months he had spent in solitary confinement was to be considered already served, so that he was immediately eligible for parole.

John Topps had originally been convicted of running away from home, an act that is not criminal. For this act and because he refused "treatment" by the DOC, he was compelled to spend three years in the Illinois penal system, of which two were in a maximum-security prison. The absurd horror of his story is most fully demonstrated by the paradox that if he had not attacked and seriously injured a guard at Sheridan, he might still be a captive of the juvenile penal system, which can keep him incarcerated until he is twenty-one; but by committing the first criminal act of his life, he was able to escape—after three years—into the saner adult prison system from which he was quickly paroled.

BETWEEN November 1971, when Judge Parsons issued his decision, and the spring of 1973, three appeals revolving around Sheridan were being briefed, argued, and decided, for the rulings of Judge White and Judge Parsons were appealed respectively to the Illinois Supreme Court and to the United States Court of Appeals for the Seventh Circuit.

While the hearing was proceeding before Judge Parsons, we had filed a class action civil-rights complaint in the federal court on behalf of all the youngsters at Sheridan, asking that the federal courts curtail the abuses there or close the institution. The Judge to whom this case was assigned, William Bauer, refused to allow the matter to proceed to trial until the Illinois Supreme Court ruled on Judge White's order. We appealed this ruling to the Court of Appeals. No decisons from any of these tribunals were forthcoming until 1973.

In the meantime, we kept contact with David Brierton, the Superintendent at Sheridan, and his eventual successor, Dennis

Wolf. We visited Sheridan on several occasions and were impressed by their attempts to improve it. The population slowly diminished—down to only forty juvenile inmates in early 1973—and conditions became much more palatable. The boys were allowed to paint their cells, hang pictures in them, and have radios or stereo equipment; the library was expanded and vocational training increased.

In early 1973, the Illinois Supreme Court finally reversed Judge White's ruling. While not denying the miserable conditions at Sheridan, the Supreme Court dismissed his rather narrow order by holding that "the Courts have traditionally accorded to correctional authorities wide discretion in matters of internal prison discipline. . . ." It seemed to be saying, don't look to the courts if you want any type of order within the institutions—a rather curious, certainly disappointing conclusion.

Within two weeks, the United States Court of Appeals affirmed Judge Parsons' decision. They reassigned all matters concerning Sheridan to Judge Bauer and pointed out that "there appears to be no valid reason for further delay in the commencement of such hearings as may be necessary in the class action." It was a pointed reminder to Judge Bauer to get on with the proceedings pending before him.

The decision by the Illinois Supreme Court, along with the ruling by the United States Court of Appeals, allowed us immediately to reopen proceedings before Judge Bauer and ask that the institution at Sheridan be closed. (The decision by the Illinois Supreme Court also gave us a clear avenue to employ the federal courts in practically any civil-rights suit against state agencies. Since the federal courts are freer of political interference than state courts, we preferred under most circumstances to try a lawsuit federally.)

Before appearing before Judge Bauer for the first hearing on the Sheridan matter, we met with Joseph Coughlin, Director of the Juvenile Division of the DOC. We insisted to him that the only circumstances under which we would settle the lawsuit would be for Sheridan to be closed to juveniles. Within three weeks, Coughlin announced that this would occur. Of course, he made no mention in his statement of our lawsuit or proposed settlement. The press release made it sound as if officials of the DOC had been planning to close Sheridan for some time. Being human, we felt a little let down that we were given no credit for this ultimate victory. On the other hand, we were too busy on other litigation to worry overlong about our bruised egos.

7

January 1972: We Revise Our Strategy

Several weeks before Judge Parsons' Sheridan trial began, Chris Dove, our social worker, had left the office; Lew Wenzell followed a month and a half after it ended. When he had come, he had promised to stay for a year but had stayed a year and a half; and now he had been offered a job as Senior Trial Attorney for the Federal Defender in San Diego. Lew and I spent an afternoon talking John Shullenberger into accepting a pay decrease and taking Lew's position. John was an excellent trial and appellate advocate who, like both Lew and me, had graduated from Northwestern University Law School and was a keen student of criminal and constitutional law. Then, since our need for a social worker had diminished, I decided to have two lawyers instead of one lawyer and a social worker, and we hired James De Zelar, who had been in the criminal law master's degree program at Northwestern and was teaching at the University of Cincinnati Law School at the time.

This changeover in the staff, and the prestige which our office was beginning to acquire—more out of fear than respect, I think—prompted us to re-evaluate our cases and the needs within the juvenile system. For the first year, the social agencies and most of the people in and around Juvenile Court had dismissed us as kooks. But the Sheridan trials, decisions, and ensuing publicity had frightened not only the Department of Corrections, but also the other agencies. And, although we failed to win the money damages in the *Armstrong* and *McIntosh* cases at the trial level, we had forced the Department of Mental Health to issue new and sane regulations on restraints. Of course, we were in the midst of appealing the cases to the Court of Appeals, and the huge damages we sought were keeping them off balance. Again, although our runaway cases were lost at the trial level, they had received huge amounts of publicity, and several times during 1971 journalists had written critical articles about how runaways were handled. Gradually, public opinion was forcing the judges to take a more enlightened position and commit less youths to jail for running away.

Lastly, the *Stanley* case about the unwed father's rights, which we had argued in the U.S. Supreme Court in October 1971 and which none of the social agencies expected us to win, was decided by the Court in our favor in early 1972. In a landmark decision, the Court held that the state of Illinois had violated the due process and equal protection rights of unwed fathers by not giving them a hearing to determine their fitness to raise their own children. The Supreme Court stated that even common-law families are protected by a veil of familial sanctity that can be pierced by the state only under unusual circumstances, and then only with a legal hearing. It went on to hold that the equal-protection rights of unwed fathers were being violated by the sexual discrimination practiced by the state.

Peter Stanley had lived with his unwed wife for eighteen years and had raised his own children, and so his case was different than many unwed fathers, but lawyers for the state interpreted the decision as holding that they must notify *any* unwed father of whom they have knowledge and give him a right to his child. This decision threw the various private and public agencies dealing with adoptions into an uproar. It was bad enough they had to assure that a mother's rights were protected; now they had to give fathers a chance as well!

These cases and the ensuing publicity caused us to be disliked and feared by the social agencies. It was irrelevant to us whether we were loved or hated, but it *was* relevant that we were feared, and that the various agencies were jumpy about which one among them we would expose or file a lawsuit against next. For several months, while we were finishing the appeals in *Armstrong* and *McIntosh* and preparing briefs for appeal in the Sheridan cases, we discussed how we could use this fear to our advantage.

The deeper we got into the juvenile quagmire, the more helpless we had felt about what went on with many, if not most, of the children, involved in the system. Most of the children hauled before the Juvenile Court of Cook County are not charged with violent criminal offenses. More than half of the cases in 1971 and 1972 involved neglect, truancy, running away from home, and technically delinquent but nonviolent actions, such as fighting (we once represented an eight-year-old girl who had squabbled with another eight-year-old girl over a dime), stealing from stores (again, we once represented a nine-year-old boy who stole cakes, cookies, and candy from a supermarket—and got sick from eating all of it), breaking windows, pulling fire alarms, etc. Many are brought to court simply because they cannot get along with their parents, others because either the police or a social worker thinks that the family is not raising the child properly and hence as a result that the child is headed for a life of crime. That this is a correct theory seems problematical. All too often, those who bring the complaints in the first place do not look at the other end of the system to see what happens to a child when he is made a ward of the state. What happens is that the child is "dumped."

After bringing the power of the state against the true parents —either through delinquency petitions theoretically aimed at children for minor delinquent acts but really aimed at bad home conditions, or through neglect petitions—and after social workers paid by the state testify against the parents, and prosecutors paid by the state argue that the child should be taken away from home because it is in his or her "best interest," the state itself, now the Kindly Parent, proceeds to neglect the child in its own parental way through a process we coined "dumping."

The Department of Children and Family Services is first appointed as the guardian for the child. This is part one of the dumping process. The Juvenile Court is mandated by statute to assure that its wards receive adequate care, custody, and training, but by statute, it may delegate that power to the DCFS in Illinois, which it often does. Once this is accomplished, the Juvenile Court conveniently forgets the kid, assuming that the DCFS can and will provide the adequate care, custody, and training.

What happens next? The case histories are monotonous in their similarity. Six or seven foster homes in one year—some good, some bad, some mediocre, along with several institutions, the Audy Home, mental-health institutions, and even prisons. The DCFS conducts no institutions of its own but relies upon the foster homes and purchase-of-care agreements with private, charitable institutions.

While the child is shunted hither and thither, his file becomes thick with useless and often contradictory data. Caseworkers use these files to substantiate their reasons for removing the child from the various foster homes and institutions and/or placing him in psychiatric hospitals, the Audy Home, or other seemingly appropriate places. Psychological tests "prove" that a child is functionally retarded, culturally retarded, potentially having a superior intelligence, manipulative, defensive, obnoxious, etc. Nothing escapes the all-seeing eye of the fact-gatherers. Body odor, bad breath, shiftiness of the eyes, stringy hair, and other trivial data concerning the child are all laid out. Ironically, many of these fact-gatherers never see the child in question, but rely upon other reports and other social workers to write up their data.

In one case, a Juvenile Court probation officer wrote a lengthy "social investigation" of a teen-age girl's home life and background but never interviewed the parents, neighbors, and teachers—because she was afraid to go into the neighborhood. The probation officer suggested that the girl (a runaway) be committed to the Department of Corrections because she was promiscuous. Ironically, this same probation officer had on several occasions attempted to seduce one of the lawyers in our office. In another case, one report in a boy's DCFS file indicated that he was violent, while most of the other data in the 250-page file indicated that he was not violent but had become a runaway because he wanted to escape from stressful situations. When he was nineteen, the state, feeling that it had run out of alternatives, had him committed to the maximum-security hospital for the criminally insane and relied upon the one report that said he had violent tendencies. In yet another case, a five-year-old boy was evaluated by a psychologist as being in need of hospitalization because:

> He appears charged with boundless energy, always discharging tension, at the motility level; constantly asking personal questions; handling and discharging everything within his reach; chewing on pencils, breaking their leads, removing their erasers, even crushing the metal part with his teeth; his chubby fingers never experienced a moment of repose—he drummed on the desk, sang rhymes, smacked his tongue, whistled, removed bits of chewed paper from his mouth and threw them at the examiner. . . .

When John Shullenberger read this last file, he came into my office and suggested that I be committed.

Each time a child is removed from one placement and put in another, there is a rationalization in the file giving excellent reasons why the move was made. The child is disturbed or retarded, and therefore needs a hospital. He or she needs controls in order to teach him discipline, and therefore should be placed with the DOC or in the Audy Home. The child is sexually promiscuous, does not respect his elders, is self-indulgent, etc., and therefore needs this placement or that. The dumping process goes on.

We realized that we would have to file lawsuits in two major areas if we were going to attempt to resolve some of these problems. At first, we thought we should litigate concerning the placement of neglected youngsters in the Audy Home, in mental-health hospitals, and in facilities for the retarded. This, we hoped, would cut off some of the dumping. But, concomitantly—and perhaps more importantly—we thought we should sue to limit the very broad jurisdiction of the juvenile justice system, which had the authority to "save" all types of children and parents whose major sin was not behavior or neglect—but poverty.

Aside from discussing what general areas we would litigate in, we had no time to define specific goals because, as we were finishing the *McIntosh* and *Armstrong* briefs, the number of children committed to the Audy Home went up dramatically. So in early 1972 we sued the Juvenile Court, the Department of Children and Family Services, and the Director of the Audy Home for allowing neglected and runaway children to be placed in that institution.

8

Detention Centers and Mental Homes for Sane and Nondelinquent Children

In most major cities, the nerve center of the juvenile system is the temporary detention center for juveniles. In Cook County, Illinois, this institution is the Arthur J. Audy Home for Children. Although it is supposed to provide only temporary shelter for children awaiting trial on delinquency charges, as a matter of fact most children there either have committed very serious criminal offenses such as murder or armed robbery or are simply runaway or "neglected." A boy or girl who has committed a run-of-the-mill offense is normally allowed to go home if his parents will accept him, so the Audy Home houses children caught at both ends of the Juvenile Court net—the very bad and those whose parents do not want them.

The old Audy Home—a new one opened in late 1973—stood about twenty-five yards behind the Juvenile Court. It was probably a decent enough building once, but decades of soot from local factories have rendered it that particular shade of urban gray—an indefinable but familiar hue halfway between depressing black and depressing gray. The building had three floors and a small yard, which is surrounded by a fifteen-foot concrete wall. "There are security measures in all sections because this is a security institution," said its Superintendent in 1969. "Each section is so keyed that no one can enter or leave that section except the people in it. And the external security features are quite visible. We have security windows, we have a wall around the yard, and I think it is pretty obvious that this is a security institution."

As with other institutions built for the care of children, the Audy Home has solitary-confinement rooms (called Blue Stone and Black Stone because of the color of the walls), approximately six feet wide and nine feet long, with the usual seatless toilet and either a metal bed attached to the wall or a mattress on the floor. There is one low-wattage bulb, which, since the children are not allowed books or magazines, is somewhat extraneous. Children in the Audy Home are subjected to various punishments for misbehavior—these include being made to run up and down stairs for thirty or forty minutes, and standing at attention for several hours. Children may write and receive letters only from their parents and may be visited only by their parents, except under unusual circumstances.

As prisons go, the Audy Home is not all that bad. Certainly it's no Sheridan. Although the punishments do seem extreme, considering the type of youngster who normally is incarcerated there, these do not usually break a child's spirit. Drugs are not used at the Audy Home. Unless a child is disturbed or upset (which seems to happen most frequently with neglected and runaway children after they have been at the Home for several months), he or she will not be punished. Life at Audy tends to be merely boring. This is how it was described in a letter smuggled out by a fourteen-year-old white boy from the suburbs, jailed because he had left home several times after being mistreated by his family.

> You get off the paddy wagon; you walk up the steps; ring the doorbell. You are told to sit; you sit, sit and you sit; you listen to the guards talk about dirty jokes at home and so forth until most leave. Then you sit, and sit and sit until the guard tells

you to stand. After you stand, he checks your hair and your jacket, your shirt, underarms, and pants, stockings. shoes, and does a very bad job of it. He takes what he finds and your belt and puts it in a big envelope. If you have cigarettes, he says he has to confiscate them, so he takes them, takes one out and lights one up and puts the rest in his top left-hand shirt pocket.

Then, you sit down again and watch him smoke your cigarettes. Then he comes over and has a form and he asks you your name, age, date of birth, father's name, mother's name, who you live with, what is the address, if you are gay, if you are to take any medicine, and if so what and when.

Then, you take that form to another guard who throws a towel in your face, points to the shower, and tells you to wipe up the floor when you are done. When you are done, he tells you to take a seat in a room. In the room there are about two dozen kids from the age of nine to eighteen, for crimes ranging from stealing three dime bars of candy to strong arm robbery or shooting a person. And all two dozen boys sit there and watch TV until 9 o'clock at night. At 9 o'clock, we get searched again as badly as before then we get in two's by height and march up to the second floor and strip and get into a bed, and you must not make a noise, if you do the guards tell you they will beat the shit out of you or put their foot up your ass. . . .

And when you go to court, you get to talk with your Public Defender for a whole two minutes, then they handcuff you to another boy and you go to court and at the court you talk to the judge, and he says if you stay or not. Then if you have to stay, they take you back to the Audy Home with the cuffs on, of course. Then, you get taken up to the section where they check you; make you strip; hang up your stuff; and put on a pair of pants, a shirt and underwear and stockings. They all got the words Audy Home on them and you go in a room and sit and watch TV until breakfast, lunch, dinner. Then sleep. They give you bed numbers. Then, you get up at 5:30 and you don't watch TV until 7 o'clock. And I guess they expect you to meditate. Then, at 7 o'clock, you eat breakfast and up here it tastes okay, but only okay. Then after breakfast, you meditate until 9 o'clock, then, the other boys go to school and you meditate until 10 o'clock, then you are taken to the school office and register for school. Then, you go to the second class for History. Then, you go to gym and you do exercises until the gym teacher's eyes get tired of watching you do them. Then, you get to play basketball. Then you go to lunch and after lunch, you meditate some more. Then, you go back to school and go to Math and then to Science and then you go back to the section to watch some TV, and also to listen to the threats of the guards and sometimes watch a threat become a reality. Then, you might go to the gym if the guards are up to it or watch TV. At 5 o'clock you eat dinner then after dinner, you watch TV or meditate. Then you go to bed at 9 o'clock and wake up at 5:30 and sit until 7 or 7:30 and eat breakfast fast and then sit until 9 o'clock, then go to school.

That is the plan as scheduled, now I will tell you what I think of this Audy Home. It does not help children, I myself am good because I don't want the shit beat out of me or stand on a wall for 10 hours with no exaggeration. When you are in here it is easy to quit smoking if you stay away from the guards for they blow smoke in your face to tease you. And the TV, what good is it, because half the time the guards watch what *they* want, and in the gym you have to exercise. They make you do so many [exercises] you don't want to play basketball or anything else. I am not saying that because I am soft, because I did exercise for an hour a night when I was home, and when you play there are two checkerboards. One shuffleboard and three basketballs for more than 75 kids. It is a fucking shame and only the big boys get to do anything for the fact that they are big and the rest are small. When you sleep if someone talks then everyone has to stand for three hours or does a few hundred knee bends.

> Even if the person is revealed, you still do the punishment. At all hours of the night you are woken up because some guards are laughing or shouting at each other or they have the TV or radio on full blast. But some guards are nice. The food is good and you eat the right things but not enough of them or anything else. You are always ashamed if you bump into someone accidentally and say you are sorry and they hit you, you can't hit back because if you do anything, that is 15 hours standing up on the wall; if you say anything for yourself, forget it, you will be on the wall until you mix with the paint. It wouldn't be so bad if it wasn't so boring and unfair. I think at Audy Home that they are very unorganized, especially the school system. It has very good teachers, but they teach only a fourth-grade level. I think in all, it would help if the people who worked there cared.

At any one time, about half the population at Audy consists of neglected children, Minors in need of Supervision, and kids between the ages of nine and twelve years who, although charged with insignificant criminal offenses, are being held in custody because the social workers thought their families are insufficient or abusive. Normally, this last group of children are on their way to having neglect petitions filed against their families. This Audy Home population of neglected and about-to-be neglected children is a shifting one. Some of the kids are there for the first time while others are between placements. Audy acts as a catchment between "dumps."

In the late 1960s, when I was still in private practice, I became interested in the Juvenile Court after having had to try one or two cases there. I became particularly interested in the "neglected" kids who appeared there, and my employer allowed me time to represent some of them. For about six months, Freddy Meinfelder, a VISTA lawyer, and I represented about twenty-five children who were in the Audy Home pursuant to neglect petitions and under the guardianship of the Children's Division of the

Cook County Department of Public Aid or the Department of Children and Family Services.

At that time, in late 1968 and early 1969, the dumping policy of this latter agency was relatively unsophisticated. If a placement could not be found for a child—whether because of bad looks, bad smell, poor intelligence, emotional problems, unpleasing personality, or simply because of a sometime discipline problem —he was just tossed in Audy until some kind of placement could be found. Neglected children were spending months, even years, locked up in Audy. It was only after we filed a law suit against the DCFS that they began to be more sensitive, or I should say shrewd, about where they dumped a child between placements. Anyway, Freddy and I wrote letters to the directors of the two agencies, asking that they remove their wards from the Audy Home. There were close to 400 children in Audy, of which almost one third were there on neglect petitions.

At the time these letters were written, lawyers had simply never been involved in juvenile proceedings, and the agencies ignored our requests. So, several weeks later, we filed lawsuits in both the state and federal courts. We used as the two named plaintiffs in the class action suits Bobby Crane and Joan Sanders, the two kids who had been at the Audy Home the longest but whose cases were not atypical of the neglected youngsters who were confined there at the time.

Bobby was about sixteen when we first met him, a fairly tall, fleshy youngster with shaggy blond hair and bright blue eyes. When he was about five years old, Bobby had been found in the Skid Row section of Chicago with a younger sister, eating from a garbage can. Not much was discovered about his background, except that his mother was probably a prostitute. The children were placed with the Children's Division, and almost immediately his mother dropped out of the picture forever. He and his sister were separated. Bobby was given a name and an age, since neither was known.

The age given to Bobby was to haunt him for years. As a social worker wrote in one of the early reports concerning him; if Bobby is seven he is retarded, if he is six he is borderline, and if he is five years old he is normal. Bobby was given the age of seven and the label of retarded. He was thus sent to an institution for the retarded where he stayed for about four years, but when he began to leave school without permission (on one of these occasions, he was involved in stealing from a local store), he was shipped back to Illinois. (Years later, he was to testify that he ran away when it dawned on him that he was different from the others at the school—he was not retarded.) In 1965, the DCFS placed him in the Audy Home for several months before putting him in a foster home. He stayed with his foster parents for six months, but violated curfew and irritated them by other acts of disobedience, so he was returned to Audy for five more months. The next "placement" was in an institution for the mentally retarded, from which he was released after several months because the staff said he was a transvestite and had homosexual tendencies. In February 1967, he was returned temporarily to the Audy Home, and two years later, when we were appointed to represent him, he was still there.

Joan Sanders was fourteen years old, although she looked much younger. She was a short, pretty, very dark and intense girl with pronounced Negro features. She had average intelligence and a nasty habit of talking back to the matrons at the Audy Home. When we were appointed to represent her, Joan had been at the Audy Home for fourteen months on a neglect petition. This confinement had left her a very hostile person. The first time I visited with Joan, she was in solitary confinement in the Blue Stone room ("the hole"), and had been there for almost three weeks. Eventually, we filed a writ of habeas corpus to remove her from this isolation.

When cases are referred to the DCFS, an Intake Unit does a study of the child and then refers the case on to the Placement Unit, which attempts to place the child. Joan had been in Audy for almost six months before her file wormed its way through the bureaucracy from the Intake to the Placement Unit. In the meantime, her condition deteriorated, and she became one of the more pronounced behavioral problems there—breaking windows, attempting suicide, fighting with the other inmates and matrons, and cursing out everybody who crossed her. By May 1969, after she had been in Audy for fifteen months, she was taken to a state mental hospital in a psychotic condition. She later told me that she had tried for about three months to be placed with either the DOC or the DMH, since she could no longer stand Audy.

Despite the fact that she was a "neglected" child whose condition had steadily worsened during an imprisonment of fifteen months, the caseworker was critical of Joan's adjustment at the Audy Home, which was considered

> unsatisfactory. She was placed in isolation much of the time because she rebelled against authority, was moody and belligerent at times and often acted as if she were a mentally ill person. When last seen by Miss Johnson on May 2, 1969, this girl advised that she had recently broken three windows in the Audy Home on April 27, 1969, and had bitten a matron on the leg. She was expected to be committed to the IYC, as this was her third delinquent act since being in the Audy Home.
>
> Joan frequently complains of being ill, and appears to be quite self-destructive. When seen by the caseworker on May 2, this girl wore bandages on her left arm, as she had cut it while hitting windows. She also had her right arm wrapped as it reportedly was sore because she had attempted to hit a matron who "squeezed" it while she was wearing handcuffs. Shortly before the termination of this contact, Joan advised Miss Johnson that she planned to break more windows or attempt to hang herself if Audy Home personnel did not allow her to sit outside.

Our lawsuits featuring Bobby and Joan, filed in the spring of 1969 in the federal and state courts, marked the first time a major litigation had been instituted on behalf of children in Illinois history, and it was an event that made the front pages of several Chicago newspapers and the editorial pages of all of them. The pressure from this publicity forced the new presiding judge of the Juvenile Division of the Circuit Court to issue an order preventing the incarceration of neglected children in the Audy Home. This order mooted out our lawsuits, and we withdrew them. We thought we had achieved a significant legal victory, and for about a year I lost contact with the Juvenile Court and the Audy Home.

After Lew and I joined the Legal Aid Society, we were so busy with the matters described in the preceding chapters that we did not have time to review the Audy Home situation. But, we did begin to notice that the number of Minor in Need of Supervision petitions against children who were wards of the Department of Children and Family Services had grown dramatically. When we looked a little closer, we found that the number of MINS children in the Audy Home had also risen dramatically. When we looked closer yet, we found that about a fifth of the kids in the Audy Home were still DCFS wards, but now were there on MINS charges. Finally, we began to notice that some of the same children whom I had represented in 1969 were back in Audy, this time as MINS. Joe Todd was one.

Joe Todd had a checkered career with the state of Illinois. When he was six, his mother having died and his father being imprisoned, he and his brother were made wards of the DCFS. They both spent time in the Audy Home while the DFCS tried to get placements for them; then he and his brother were together in a private children's orphanage and several foster homes. They were thrown out of the orphanage after they climbed up on the roof and started playing with television antennas, and the foster parents claimed they could not cope with Joe's hyperactivity. After another stay at Audy, the DCFS shipped Joe down to one of the institutions in Texas from which it purchases care. Joe stayed in Texas until he was ten. He enjoyed life there, particularly since during one year he did not go to school, having been taken out for alleged mischievous conduct and put to work on one of the ranches run by the institution. He liked working around the stables, riding horses, and hiking in the country, but several times he made mistakes for which he paid dearly. Once he stayed away from the institution for too long and was made to work on a road gang with other boys—and for an entire day he was made to do this work with only his undershorts on. Besides being embarrassed by the stares of passers-by, he became extremely ill from sunburn. Several months later, he killed a dog, and after being chained to his bed and made to wear the dog's tail around his neck for two weeks, he was shipped back to the DFCS and to the Audy Home. That was where I first met him in 1969. He was a brown-haired Tom-Sawyer type of boy—bright, alert, and personable.

After Judge White issued his order, Joe was placed in Chicago State Mental Hospital. The fact that he was not in need of psychiatric care and the fact that the social worker in charge of him at Chicago State complained for two years to the DCFS that the boy was not in need of hospitalization did not bother the agency. Once he was in Chicago State, no one had to worry about placing him: let the DMH worry about him now. When Lew and I, at the Legal Aid Society, discovered Joe at Chicago State in 1970, we were able to pressure the agency into putting him into a fairly good private child-care facility on Chicago's North Side. Joe lasted there more than a year, but ran away several times—which caused the institution to dump him back with DCFS which, of course, returned him to the Audy Home.

While at Audy, Joe ended up in isolation on several occasions. Eventually, after a huge, 225-pound guard had taunted him (he was then only fourteen and weighed about 100 pounds) and he struck the guard, the Audy authorities became eager to get rid of him. With the approval of the DCFS, they filed delinquency charges against Joe for hitting the guard. Now Joe was a "difficult placement problem," since he had been in several institutions and foster homes as well as a mental hospital, the DOC appeared appropriate to DCFS caseworkers. Fearing that the trial judge might think there was no alternative but to go along with this recommendation, we tried to act as expeditiously as possible. Several days after the delinquency charges were filed—this was in March 1972—we filed a federal civil-rights suit against the Audy Home, the Juvenile Court, and the DCFS, with Joe as a plaintiff representing all DCFS children in the Audy Home. The case was assigned to the Honorable Philip Tone, newly appointed to the federal bench.

Judge Tone looked every bit the Hollywood version of a federal judge—fiftyish, with bright blue eyes, craggy features, and a shock of graying hair. He came from one of Chicago's most prestigious law firms and had helped to write several model state and federal laws. We filed for a preliminary injunction to limit punishment at the Audy Home, and the hearing on this motion was granted.

During the three-day hearing before Judge Tone, we put children on the stand to testify about various punishments employed at Audy: running up and down stairs, standing at attention in the hallways, being locked in solitary confinement. But beyond this they testified about being degraded by members of the staff, and they described at great length the boredom of the Audy Home (they mentioned the interminable hours of television, but pointed out that they were not allowed to watch the news programs or read newspapers) and the complete lack of recreation. Audy Home authorities denied these allegations, but after the hearing Judge Tone called us into his chambers and indicated that he was going to rule in our favor unless the Audy Home and the DCFS worked out an agreement to eliminate some of the worse aspects of life there. After several weeks of bargaining, we agreed to dismiss our lawsuit when several of our demands were met. The Audy Home agreed to eliminate the punishment of running up and down stairs and to limit standing at attention to no more than forty-five minutes. The Juvenile Court agreed that probation officers would visit their clients at the Audy Home at least once a week, and any child in the Audy Home for more than two weeks would have to be returned to court with a supervisor's report explaining why the continued residence was necessary. The DCFS caseworkers had to visit their DCFS wards in the Audy Home once a week and the supervisor testify every two weeks why it was necessary for any one of them to be there. Under no circumstances could any child remain in the Audy Home more than two months. At that point we had resolved the Audy Home issue as much as it could be resolved through legal maneuvers. As for Joe, the Department put him back in the institution he had last run away from—a stopgap measure, but the only one available.

Although the newspapers and television commentators claimed that we had won this second Audy Home case, we were experienced enough by now to realize that we had not. By poking around the Audy Home mess again, we uncovered an even more ghastly can of worms: the dumping of neglected children in institutions for the mentally disturbed and retarded. Indeed, we began to understand that each time we looked into a new area of alleged abuse, we were almost certain to find several other horrible abuses connected with it. It was not cynicism that caused us never to rejoice in a "victory" but acceptance of the old Russian saying that a pessimist is merely a well-informed optimist.

THE FACT WAS, whenever we put pressure on one juncture in the dumping process, the population in the other junctures would increase. After our original Audy Home suit in 1970, I visited Elgin State Mental Hospital and discovered, for instance, that of twenty-four preadolescent youngsters on one ward, twenty-one were under the guardianship of the DCFS and had been at the

Audy Home when Judge White signed his order releasing neglected youngsters from that institution. We were later to discover that several hundred DCFS wards from Cook County were in public mental-health hospitals in and around Chicago. We were convinced that many, if not most, of these DCFS wards did not belong in mental-health facilities. The appalling thing was that once they got there, they tended to stay longer than children who were *not* wards of the state, because parents would take their kids out of a mental hospital as soon as it seemed feasible, while the DCFS workers tended to forget about their wards, believing that they were now the responsibilities of the DMH.

How did all these neglected youngsters get into the hospitals, when they were not in need of psychiatric care? In Illinois, like most states, the mental-health code allowed parents or guardians to put their children in mental-health facilities whether or not the child agreed to be so committed. Adults are entitled to a hearing if they object the commitment. The DCFS took advantage of this provision, particularly after the Audy Home was to a great extent unusable for dumping purposes.

Rather than attack the statute that allowed children to be detained against their will in mental hospitals, *and* attack the DCFS for dumping innocent children in institutions for the disturbed and retarded, *and* attack the DMH for giving such bad care to youngsters who legitimately belonged in those facilities, we decided to approach the three issues one step at a time. We started by filing a lawsuit in the Circuit Court of Cook County asking that that court declare the statute unconstitutional because it violated the children's rights to the due processes and equal protection of the laws. We argued that the constitutional due-process clause mandated that any individual put in a mental-health facility must be granted a fair hearing if he objected. There was plenty of precedent to support us on this point, and we added that it would be a denial of equal protection for the courts to grant hearings for adults but not to children.

This case was assigned to the Honorable Joseph Schneider in the Law Division of the Circuit Court of Cook County. We had become inured to the ways of state court judges, and their susceptibility to political pressures (they are elected periodically and rely upon the political organizations to keep them in office, whereas federal judges have a lifetime tenure), but Judge Schneider, like Judge White, proved to be a man of intelligence and integrity.

Although the Department of Mental Health was the prime Defendant, through their counsel, Jerry Goldberg, they sided with us, while the DCFS filed briefs arguing that children had no rights such as we wished to claim for them. But Judge Schneider ruled in February 1972 that the state's interpretation of the statute was unconstitutional, and that minors of thirteen and over were entitled to sign themselves out of private and public mental health hospitals and that, if the state objected, they were entitled to a judicial hearing within five days of the objection. If the child were indigent, he was to be afforded free counsel and a free transcript of proceedings.

Instead of closing the case there, Judge Schneider kept it open and asked us to monitor the circumstances under which DCFS wards were allowed to sign themselves out. For the next several months, with the help of some student investigators, we informed the DCFS wards in mental hospitals of their right to a hearing: Elgin State Hospital, about thirty miles west of Chicago, Chicago-Read Mental Health Center, on Chicago's North Side, and the Tinley Park Mental Health Center, about twenty miles south of the city. There were many DCFS wards in private hospitals, but we simply did not have the resources to reach them. The DMH also complied with Judge Schneider's order and told each child of his right to release and/or a hearing and prominently displayed notices in the children's wards.

Quickly, the expected snag developed. As each child signed himself out and the DMH notified the DCFS that he had done so (and, moreover, that he or she was not in need of mental-health treatment in the first place), the response of the DCFS was clear: So what? Judge Schneider's order rapidly became a hollow ruling. A fourteen-year-old child cannot simply take up his suitcases and rush out on the sidewalk with nowhere to go. The DCFS did nothing. Soon the children got their message and withdrew their requests to leave.

After interviewing staff members at the three hospitals involved, we filed a petition for additional relief before Judge Schneider. According to officials with the DMH, at least 80 per cent of the DCFS wards at Chicago-Read Center were not in need of psychiatric care, and at the other two hospitals, the figures were about 65 per cent. Judge Schneider ordered an immediate hearing, and in July 1972 we presented testimony from the mental-health workers. The state countered with testimony from the Director of the Chicago region of the DCFS.

Reviewing the evidence, Judge Schneider observed that "in a substantial number of cases, it appeared that once a child was hospitalized, there was little contact by the guardian, DCFS, with its wards or even with the staff involved in the treatment at the hospital. . . ." "It is an awesome responsibility for the Court to remove a child from its natural family, and when this is done, there is a duty upon the State to adequately care for the child. Governmental neglect and inadequacies are no more sacred or legally justifiable than parental neglect and inadequacies when they jeopardize the health and welfare of the child." Judge Schneider then appointed our office as attorney and child advocate for all wards of the DCFS who were or would be hospitalized in private or public mental-health facilities, until further order of the court. He ordered both agencies to report to the court and ourselves every month concerning any child in any mental-health institution, to state why the child was in the hospital, for how long, and whether or not he needed mental-health care.

The most important aspect of this second order by Judge

Schneider was his appointing our office as attorney and child advocate for the children. Equally important was the fact that he ordered us to bring to him for review any abuses we discovered in our representation of these children. From August 1972 to September 1973, we appeared before him a dozen times with new lawsuits challenging certain treatment, care, and state regulations which we thought violated the children's statutory and/or constitutional rights. On several occasions, we sought, and received, court orders directing the DCFS immediately to remove specific children from the public mental hospitals and to purchase care for them at private hospitals, inasmuch as the DMH could not give them what they needed. In two cases, for instance, girls requiring security and treatment were locked in solitary confinement twenty-four hours at a time because there were no security facilities for girls who required hospitalization.

Attorneys for the DCFS tried to stop us from interviewing clients whom it had taken out of public facilities and put in private ones. They argued that once the children were no longer in the state hospitals, we no longer had a right to determine under what circumstances they received care, and they instructed the private hospitals to have no contact with us and to give us no material. (For good reason, too: in one case they tried to cover up, we discovered a girl with above-average intelligence in a private institution for the mentally retarded, while in another, we discovered that the DCFS was paying $70 a day to a private institution where we were told by the staff, among other points of expert advice, that our client should hire a pimp and become a prostitute to satisfy her sexual drives.) Judge Schneider quickly undid this log jam.

AS OUR investigation continued we discovered new and worse abuses. One of the worst came to our attention almost immediately and it involved one of my favorite former clients, Bobby Crane.

In 1970, when Bobby was released from his two and a half years at the Audy Home, the DCFS put him in the Elgin State Hospital. (The social worker's classification of Bobby as "retarded" when he was gratuitously given the age of seven was still haunting him.) Because he was a minor (he was then fifteen), Bobby had no right to decide for himself whether he wanted to be there, and he had no right to a hearing to determine if he should be. The agency simply dropped him into the institution, as they did with countless others, and forgot about him. He had no parents or relatives either, so he stayed at Elgin for the next three years. The fact that most of the caseworkers who worked with him thought he didn't need psychiatric care really did not mean much. The man who worked most closely with Bob considered him neither retarded nor disturbed, but suffering from a lack of judgment due to "socio-retardation." By this Gary Olsen meant that Bobby's background of institutionalization, combined with the deprivation he suffered during the first years of his life, had left him with a need for immediate gratification, a need which caused him to act impulsively.

When Bobby became eighteen, he was transferred out of the Children and Adolescent Program at Elgin and placed in the Adult Program. The differences between these two programs were minimal. The major therapy was still "chemotherapy" and so-called behavioral modification. But Olsen had worked hard with Bobby for two years, and it was a setback for the boy to lose this important relationship.

Bobby had been in the adult unit for about two months when he ran away from Elgin once or twice and then stole some papers from the superintendent's office. Within two days, he was on his way to the Illinois State Security Hospital in Chester. (I had lost track of Bobby after our first lawsuit against the Audy Home, and did not immediately know about his transfer from Elgin to Chester.)

Chester was one of those institutions which gladdened the hearts of the officials we had dealt with at Sheridan: it was probably the only institution in Illinois which was worse. It had been a prison for over a century, and then, in the early 1960s, it was transferred to the DMH and its name changed from "prison" to "hospital." The inmates at the Security Hospital were primarily men committed there by criminal courts after they had been adjudicated incompetent to stand trial or not guilty of serious felonies by reason of insanity, also men who had allegedly committed criminal acts while at state mental hospitals or with the adult division of the DOC. As of January 1, 1972, Chester had 291 inmates. Of these, 113 had been charged with assaultive behavior, 77 with murder or attempted murder, 31 with sexual offenses, and 27 for robbery. In short, Chester housed the most violently and seriously psychotic patients in the state of Illinois, and as a result it boasted the greatest security of any mental-health facility, greater in many respects than most prisons.

Bobby was nineteen when he was transferred to Chester, and for its purposes was classified as an adult, but there were also eighteen boys between the ages of thirteen and seventeen at the institution. Bobby and the other boys were intermingled with inmates twice their age, and lived in cellblocks housing between forty and sixty men. Each cellblock is separated from the others by one double-keyed heavy steel door, constantly attended by a turnkey. The cellblocks are pretty much the same throughout Chester—in fact, about the same as those in most prisons. The usual upper gallery of steel-barred cells is used for solitary confinement and overlooks the main living area, in the middle of which huddle a few chairs, a table, and a television set. At one end of the unit are the toilet and washing facilities (the toilets are seatless and are not separated by partitions.) In the main area, there is also a "nursing station," a wire-enclosed cage containing the medicines and tranquilizing drugs that are administered four times a day. On the main floor of the gallery are the steel-barred cells—five by nine feet, with a bunk bed and a bucket of water (used as a toilet during the hours when the inmates are locked up).

In some of the cellblocks a wooden basketball backboard was set up on the railing between the first and second galleries. This backboard was used for games when there was a "recreational therapist" around, which wasn't often. We were at Chester one time when the inmates had one of these "basketball therapy" sessions. Table and chairs were pushed off to one side and six or seven inmates, obviously drugged to capacity, tried to play basketball—a horrifying farce, an ugly slow-motion charade of what the game should have been, with none of the players able to get the ball even close to the basket.

Among other minors at Chester was a fifteen-year-old boy who had been transferred there from the DOC. Like most of the other inmates, he was subjected to "chemotherapy," that euphemistic term for the uncontrolled use of drugs. Chemotherapy was even more in evidence at Chester than at Sheridan, where it was given only to those in solitary confinement. The "patients" at Chester were in a constant stupefaction, a state characterized by their glassy, red-eyed stares and extremely slow motions. Our fifteen-year-old boy received a daily dosage of initially 1400 milligrams of Thorazine, later 1000 milligrams. He was also given a daily 64 milligrams of Trilafon, 20 milligrams of Valium, 8 milligrams of Artane, 2 grains of Empiral, and 2 grains of phenobarbital.

Thorazine was our old friend from Sheridan. Valium was a milder tranquilizer, intended to relieve symptoms and anxiety resulting from stressful circumstances—Chester was certainly stressful. According to the manufacturer it was of no value in treating psychotic patients and should not be employed in lieu of appropriate treatement. Trilafon was an extremely potent tranquilizer and antinausea agent used to control anxiety, tension, overactivity, and emotional disorders. (Some of the side effects are protrusion, discoloration, aching and rounding of the tongue, tight feeling in the throat, slurred speech, muscle weakness, blurred vision, and dry mouth. According to the manufacturer, the dosage must be individualized and adjusted according to the severity of the condition and response obtained; prolonged administration of doses exceeding 24 milligrams daily should be reserved for hospitalized patients or patients under observation.) The other drugs were primarily used to counteract the side effects of these three. As one of our medical experts later testified, some of the drugs were given to keep the Chester inmates drugged, some to counteract these tranquilizers, and others to counteract the adverse side effects of the counteractants.

When I discovered that Bobby had been committed to Chester, I was shocked. Bobby had never been violent, and, in fact, he reacted to stress by running away. During all his years of institutionalization, the fights he had gotten into could be counted on the fingers of one hand. We immediately phoned our old friend the DMH counsel, Jerry Goldberg, who in turn called Chester and got the story of how Bobby had been transferred there after apparently running away from Elgin and breaking into the superintendent's office.

Within a week, we filed a petition for declaratory judgment, asking Judge Schneider to declare Bobby's transfer to a maximum-security, prisonlike institution in violation of his rights to the due processes of the law. We demanded that Bobby be returned from Chester immediately and that the court order the DCFS to give him adequate care. Judge Schneider ordered Bobby brought back to Elgin, pending the outcome of the lawsuit, and called for an immediate hearing.

The two major defendants in the case—the superintendent, and the part-time psychiatrist who prescribed all the drugs at Chester—were "too ill" to attend the hearings. But the Director of the Child and Adolescent programs for the Department of Mental Health and the Director of the Institute for Juvenile Research—the first a noted child psychologist, and the second a respected child psychiatrist—both testified as to the need for Chester (both for adults and children), the feasibility of Bobby's transfer, and the fact that Chester, though not perfect, was a decent maximum-security institution. On cross-examination, they were both forced to admit that Chester could not be certified even as a hospital, much less a mental-health hospital, and that they knew almost nothing about it, each having been there only once. Both admitted that there was no full-time psychiatrist on the staff, and the Director of the Institute for Juvenile Research was also forced to concede that none of the three full-time Board-certified psychiatrists who worked for him (paid by the DMH) had ever donated even one minute to the children institutionalized in the DMH facilities. Their duties were to teach full time at the University of Illinois Schools of Medicine and Social Work, and the Director was forced to admit that most of the doctors coming from those schools worked in private practice and, hence, did nothing to help the children unfortunate enough to rely upon the public sector for assistance.

We subpoenaed several professional workers at Chester who testified candidly about the deplorable conditions there. Gary Olsen—despite his superiors at Elgin being highly critical of his testimony, which contradicted that of the two directors—testified that Bobby did not belong in a security institution. Bobby himself spoke quietly and effectively about his troubled history, his stay at Elgin, and his imprisonment at Chester.

After mulling over the testimony for several days, Judge Schneider entered his third precedent-setting decision in the series that had begun when he gave children the right to a hearing upon commitment to mental-health facility. His lengthy oral opinion was extremely critical of both the DCFS and the DMH:

> In reviewing the evidence, the first transfer from the adolescent unit to the adult unit at Elgin may have been questionable

in light of the testimony. However, the capricious and punitive transfer [of Bobby] to the Illinois Security Hospital from Elgin . . . by no stretch of the imagination, by no stretch of the testimony, could be considered as a permissible or reasonable decision. It seems to me that it was a shocking disregard of the most fundamental constitutional right of due process, and if we think of what due process is, it is really no more than the right to be treated fairly.

The Illinois Security Hospital is a mental hospital to treat the most dangerous and violently ill persons. The evidence shows by no criteria that [Bobby] belonged at the Illinois Security Hospital. There is no program for adolescents there. The average age of the patients at the Illinois Security Hospital was between twenty-eight and thirty.

By diagnosis . . . over 200 suffered from schizophrenia. Forty-four were paranoid. Fifteen were mentally retarded. . . .

The reason for [Bobby's] transfer is quite unclear. But that the most one could say is, he was there because of running away or petty theft.

The Illinois Security Hospital has never been an accredited hospital. . . . Everyone admits that the physical condition is revolting and, in my opinion, degrading to the individual. . . .

It is questionable whether any individual, much less [Bobby] —and I am making these comments because of my concern, perhaps, as a citizen, as well as a judge, about conditions at Chester—but it is questionable whether it is limited to [Bobby]; it is questionable whether [Bobby] could get adequate treatment, even fit treatment under those conditions.

It is not related to this case, but again I must express some concern as a citizen that our society is given a false sense of security by having a hospital named the Illinois Security Hospital. This false sense of security is that treatment is actually being given to the violent, dangerous, and mentally ill. . . .

In light of what has transpired in this case, the order that I wish to be prepared and entered in this case is that the transfer from Elgin to the Illinois Security Hospital was unconstitutional. . . .

Several weeks after Judge Schneider's decision, he entered a written order which held that no patient could be transferred to Chester without a hearing by a "special review committee." The committee was to consist of at least three experienced mental-health professionals, one of whom would be a Board-eligible psychiatrist. No member of the committee could ever have been involved with, or engaged in, the direct care of the particular patient, or even have any connection with the unit from which the patient was to be transferred. Before the transfer, the committee would have to notify the patient, his attorney, parents or relatives, legal guardian if any, as well as his legal custodian and any other person selected by the patient or the other persons mentioned, of the time and place of the hearing and of their right to be present. The patient was to be entitled to be represented by counsel, and, if he had no attorney, the facility was to contact the public defender and request representation for the patient. The patient's attorney was to have an opportunity to review any relevant records, consult with the client, and talk to witnesses before the hearing. A written transcript of the proceedings was to be made and made available to the patient and his attorney. Before any transfer was approved, all available alternatives, including transfer to another program within the same facility, must be considered. If a transfer were recommended, the committee was to put in writing the reasons for it, a treatment plan setting forth what the committee expected could be accomplished by it, and the estimated length of time the patient was expected to be at the security hospital or the maximum-security unit.

Several months later, in another case we filed before Judge Schneider, he ruled that persons under eighteen could not be sent to Chester. Judge Schneider ordered the DCFS to provide Bobby with adequate care immediately. But the DCFS did not act immediately in Bobby's case, and we had to go back to Judge Schneider several more times, seeking orders against the DCFS to take care of Bobby. During one ludicrous period, when Bobby was living at a YMCA and the DCFS agreed to pay his room and board as well as a few dollars a day spending money, its attorneys told us it would take six weeks for their vouchers to be approved and for the money to get to him. Of course, neither Bobby nor the YMCA could manage on the six-week potential promise, so various people, including his DCFS caseworker and lawyers in our office, ended up bankrolling Bobby for three weeks while the bureaucratic wheels ground slowly on. Finally, Bobby was placed in a foster home with a small allowance. However, we were to encounter additional difficulties with Bobby's placement during the ensuing months.

BY JANUARY 1973, we had discovered how to keep track of the disgraceful procedures by which neglected children from the Audy Home were dumped—first in facilities for the emotionally disturbed and ultimately in Chester. It was involved, intricate, and exhausting work, which included long hours of legal research, writing briefs, and haggling with state's lawyers before Judge Schneider to get access to information. The most difficult part was the hours spent investigating the institutions and interviewing the children. Several times we almost had to give up because we simply didn't have enough money or manpower to keep going, and when we sought assistance from various foundations and schools of social work we were turned down. Ultimately, the Playboy Foundation gave us the funding we needed to hire social-work and law students!

The more we investigated and the more we talked with the kids, the more we became convinced that we were only scratching the surface. More and more stories reached us about abuses of Illinois children in out-of-state institutions and the placement of nonretarded youngsters in homes for the retarded.

Christmas came and went, and it was New Year's, 1973. John,

Jim, and I spent increasingly long hours in the cold, dark evenings discussing strategy for investigating and litigating these additional dumping grounds. Actually, we had been through it many times before and knew how to go about it; I am sure that subconsciously we were simply buying more time. We did not especially look forward to the exhausting battles which lay ahead. There would be days and nights of investigations and research, hours spent hassling, threatening, and bullying state officials, time wasted sloshing through the snow to court and waiting for the case to be called—only to have it postponed by the state's lawyers. And always there were the nightmares in the institutions themselves. After fortifying ourselves with a great deal of Scotch one icy, gusty January evening, we decided it was time to proceed.

9

How to Dump Homeless Children in Out-of-the-Way Places

BEGINNING in the late 1960s and until 1973, the state of Illinois had placed hundreds of children each year in Texas institutions. By 1973, there were more than 500 Illinois DCFS children in Texas. We had often heard rumors about various abuses at the Texas places but had been too busy with other matters to investigate the allegations seriously. During our investigation after Judge Schneider's order, however, we uncovered several unsettling facts that prompted us to file suit challenging Illinois' right to place neglected children in Texas.

While routinely investigating the files of DCFS youngsters at Chicago-Read Mental Health Center, we discovered that one young girl had been sterilized in November 1971. We looked into the matter further and discovered that this occurred at a Texas institution near Austin. After badgering DCFS officials a bit more, we uncovered documents which indicated that the girl had originally undergone exploratory surgery, but that during the operation the doctors had performed the hysterectomy, cutting out the uterus and both ovaries. After surgery, the DCFS and Meridell officials told both the girl and her father that she had received an appendectomy. Two months later, she was sent back to Chicago, and placed in Chicago-Read hospital. Four months after *that,* when she had not had her period for six months, mental-health workers told Denise Wade and her father the truth about the hysterectomy.

We tried to obtain the medical records of the surgery, but the DCFS refused to give them to us, saying we had no right to them. Ultimately, after conferences between Judge Schneider, the DCFS's attorneys, and ourselves, DCFS did give us some medical records which described the operation, and these showed that during the operation—in which an appendectomy was performed—the surgeons found a teratoma on one of the ovaries and decided to remove both ovaries and the uterus because of a fear of malignancy. However, one of the DCFS attorneys told us there was no pathologist's report to indicate whether or not the ovary with the teratoma was indeed malignant.

We asked several gynecologists about the operation, and they all agreed that teratomas do sometimes indicate a malignancy and that if it would be necessary to remove one ovary, it might be best to remove both at the same time. All of them thought, though, that during such an operation a gynecologist should be present. According to records, it appeared that none was.

As lawyers we had several questions concerning the surgery. First and foremost, was it necessary? Also, were adequate tests performed to determine in advance whether or not the teratoma was malignant? Was it necessary to perform the hysterectomy without, apparently, getting permission from the DCFS or the girl's father? Why was the girl not brought back to Illinois for the surgery? Why was there no social worker from DCFS with the girl during the surgery? And why did nobody from DCFS ever tell the father and the girl the facts? Of course, the father and girl were both poor and black, and the father was treated with the usual cavalier attitude that caseworkers adopt with parents who are forced to admit to "neglect" in order to get help for their children.

Denise had been in trouble in school and had allegedly run away from home twice. After spending some time at the Audy Home, her father admitted to "neglect" so that his child could receive the care she so desperately needed, according to the Juvenile Court. First, she was placed in several foster homes, and then she was sent to the facility in Texas. One week after the girl's thirteenth birthday, the hysterectomy occurred. She was back at Chicago in Chicago-Read Mental Health Center by March 1972, and she was still languishing there in December, when we obtained the information about the hysterectomy.

When we first questioned DCFS lawyers about the facts, they told us that permission for the hysterectomy was obtained from the Guardianship Administrator of the DCFS during the operation, and that a pathologist's report indicated that the ovaries were, indeed, malignant. But though we tried to get copies of the telegram and the pathologist's report over the next several months, we were constantly put off. Finally, we filed suit to obtain complete reports and for an order placing Denise in a private hospital under the care of Dr. Marvin Schwarz and two professors of gynecology and neurology. The Court did order the DCFS to hand over all medical files, and DCFS officials agreed to place the girl with Dr. Schwarz and our other specialists. As it turned out, there *was* a pathologist's report, and, as we suspected, it indicated that no malignancy existed. Still, this did not necessarily mean that the operation was uncalled for. The Texas hospital hired a Chicago counsel and balked at giving us additional information. So in the fall of 1973 we turned the case over to a Chicago law firm specializing in personal injury cases so that a suit could be initiated against the DCFS, the Texas institution, and the hospital.

Denise's hysterectomy prompted us to look more closely at the Texas institutions. And other events prompted us to file our lawsuit demanding that Illinois take its children out of these Texas facilities.

Brad Stewart was a tall, slender, good-looking sixteen-year-old with shoulder-length hair. In the fall of 1972, he had been placed in an east Texas institution, where he stayed for four months before escaping and thumbing his way back to Chicago. While in Texas, he attended classes, but at an eighth-grade level, because there was no high school on the grounds. He had been in his second year of high school in Chicago. Subsequent investigation revealed that there were sixty youngsters at the center, about half of whom were adolescents and only one of whom attended high school. The others did a lot of "make-work" jobs like digging drainage ditches and mopping floors. Of the sixty children in the institution, more than fifty were from Chicago.

The children lived in dormitory rooms, between five and fifteen in each, with the girls and boys segregated in two separate buildings about a half a mile apart. To keep discipline, it was not uncommon for the staff to handcuff a child to a tree or a bench for an hour or more. Also, the inmates could be paddled with a large board for infractions of the rules, or be placed in a "disciplinary room."

In early December, Brad tried to run away from this institution. After he was apprehended, he was brought back and put in the "confinement room." This small chamber was not actually solitary confinement, since several children might be in it together and, in fact, during the two weeks Brad was confined there, there were sometimes as many as three other boys with him. There was no toilet and the boys had to pound on the door to get a staff member to let them use a toilet down the hall. Frequently, they simply had to relieve themselves on the floor. During the first two days of his December confinement, Brad was handcuffed to another boy; when he was first brought back to the institution, he was made to strip and was paddled on his legs, arms, back, buttocks, and genitals by the director.

In February 1973, Brad was again placed in the confinement room, this time for fighting. Again he was made to strip and was beaten until he could not stand. After that, he was kept in the room, handcuffed to another boy, for ten days; the boys were given no change of clothes and were not allowed to shower; there were no beds. Finally, another inmate slipped a key under the door, and Brad got the cuffs off, and after removing a wooden panel on the wall and knocking his way through the plaster managed to get into an adjoining room. He escaped from the institution and hitchhiked back to Chicago.

After talking to DCFS caseworkers and several other youngsters who had been in the same institution and who corroborated Brad's story, we filed a lawsuit in the Circuit Court of Cook County against the DCFS, asking the Court to order it to remove all children from the Texas center. A hearing was ordered, but the recently appointed Director of the DCFS, agreed with our facts and ordered all state wards removed from the institution within three weeks.

After we thought we had settled the case, Jim De Zelar had to go to Texas to investigate some of the other facilities there. He discovered that the three largest institutions where children were placed had interlocking boards of directors, and that approximately 70 per cent of the kids were wards of the Juvenile Court of Cook County and the Illinois DCFS. In Texas! Illinois was paying about $23 per day per child at two of these places and $18 at the third—during the fiscal years of 1972 and 1973, more than $3 million all told. Despite this tremendous amount of money from Illinois, the lack of services offered was glaring. Where was all the money going? The specter of possible political shenanigans raised its head.

All three of the institutions employed wilderness programs, operations in which boys were sent camping to learn ranger techniques of survival. However, these camping trips lasted as long as three years for some of the boys, during which time they did not go to school and were subject to military-style discipline. (Several of the boys caught smoking at one of the camps were made to eat a pack-and-a-half of cigarettes and then run for a mile. One of the youths reported that when he threw up, the counselors made him stick his face into the vomit.) When Jim asked at one of the camps what formal educational experience the boys were receiving, the director pointed out that they had to read the Boy Scout manual. Punishments included being confined to one's tent for as long as a week, being led around with a rope around one's neck if one tried to run away, being made to stand in tubs of cold water for several hours, and having one's hair shaved off for offenses such as smoking. In one of the camps for girls, there were three metal cages into which the girls could be placed for punishment.

When Jim returned, he wrote a lengthy report on the Texas situation which we forwarded to the DCFS. Although the new director, Dr. Jerome Miller, appeared to be sincere in wanting to remove the Illinois children from the Texas operations, we began to feel, as time went on, that his staff who were liaison to these institutions were sabotaging his efforts. When it appeared that one of his lawyers erred about the existence of a pathology report in Denise's case, our patience was exhausted, and we refiled petitions before Judge White asking him to order the DCFS to remove all of the Illinois children within thirty days or explain to the Juvenile Court and to us why each child should stay. Of course, we were not necessarily asking that they remove all the children, merely those who did not belong there, and that they explain to the Court in detail on what grounds the other children remained.

In familiar fashion, the DCFS acted with a haste that bordered on the paranoid. During July and August, it took children out wholesale from the Texas institutions—and we were not too sure where they were being put, except that the population of the Audy Home and certain psychiatric institutions coincidentally increased. Before Judge White, we asked for an order on the DCFS to give us the name of each child removed from Texas institutions during July and August of 1973 and the DCFS's plans concerning them. Judge White's order to this effect made it much easier for us to monitor exactly what the DCFS was doing with the 500 kids.

IN OUR WORK, we had been in many jails, hospitals, and detention centers. As many times as I went to a Sheridan or a Chester, I could never walk away without a feeling of severe depression at the thought of what some humans would do to others in the name of "help." Some of the institutions in Texas were equally depressing, although admittedly better than Sheridan or Chester. But of all the places we went to, the homes for retarded children made us most despondent.

In the large state schools of Illinois, like Lincoln and Dixon, you can walk through ward after ward for the profoundly retarded, and see row after row of young people in their teens and early twenties, wrapped in diapers, who are just barely existing at a vegetable level. There are six-year-old hydrocephalics and children with no faces and no limbs, who have merely existed for years on tube-feeding. Sometimes, only one or two workers are responsible for a ward of thirty or forty children and/or adults with the minds of babies, or with no apparent minds at all. Even in the worst of these institutions, you admire those people, for they work day in and day out at difficult and seemingly unrewarding labor.

While we were investigating conditions of the DCFS wards in mental hospitals, pursuant to Judge Schneider's order, and at about the same time that we encountered the problems in Texas, we stumbled on one of the most disgusting practices of the state in its care of neglected children. One of our investigators visited the Lincoln State School for the Retarded in downstate Illinois. This mammoth institution housed more than 2500 retarded individuals of all ages. Twenty DCFS wards were at the institution, and the DCFS had told us that since they were so retarded it was impossible to give them any hearing. Our investigator found otherwise. He spoke to the youngsters who were not profoundly retarded, and to the staff at Lincoln. According to the latter, half of the children did not belong at Lincoln because they weren't retarded. Learning difficulties, cultural retardation, and physical deficiencies made them "difficult to place," but that is hardly the same.

For three months, we badgered the DCFS to remove the ten children from Lincoln with no success. Finally, we filed a supplemental complaint before Judge Schneider, asking him to order that the kids be removed and to draw up guidelines that would prevent the placement of a child in an institution for the retarded until he had been screened. Within a week, the DCFS had removed the ten youngsters and asked Judge Schneider to dismiss the suit as moot. Moreover, it argued, we were supposed to be representing only those youngsters in institutions for the emotionally disturbed, not children in institutions for the retarded. Judge Schneider quickly clarified his original decision: we were to represent children in both categories. He also ordered a hearing to determine whether there should be screening processes before kids could be placed in a home for the retarded.

While preparing for this hearing before Judge Schneider, we investigated more files of the many youngsters in facilities for the retarded. The horrors multiplied. We discovered that these children were dumped not only into state institutions, but into private facilities for the retarded as well. And we were certain that many of the youngsters were in any case not retarded at all. The file of one girl, Victoria Murray, interested us particularly.

Victoria's file indicated that she had come to the United States at the age of fourteen from Jamaica, and had worked as a domestic for several years before being enrolled in a suburban high school. According to the file, she was forced out of the high school by authorities who felt that she should be under the guardianship of the state. She was an abrasive person, the file reported, who had assaulted DCFS caseworkers and police officers and who ended up in the Audy Home and Elgin State Mental Hospital.

DCFS papers also revealed that she had a rather low IQ (in the 70's), that she was emotionally and/or mentally disturbed, with an hysterical personality, suffered from culture shock, may have been retarded, and was a "teen-age autocrat." The sources for all of these diagnoses appeared to have been several DCFS caseworkers, an Elgin social worker, and an Elgin psychologist. Apparently, Victoria had been at Elgin when Judge Schneider signed his order allowing hearings. She insisted upon such a hearing, and when staff workers stated that she never belonged there in the first place, she was released. The DCFS promptly deposited her in an institution for the retarded in Missouri, apparently because of her low IQ.

Two things especially interested us about Victoria's file. First, assuming that her IQ score reflected her true intelligence, it was not that of a "retarded" child but of one who is, according to psychologists, "dull-normal." But this was not the real point. We had come to distrust IQ tests almost completely, especially in the case of kids from racial minorities. The IQ tests were standardized in the 1930s, 1940s, and 1950s on white middle-class children, and they are still often given in group settings in the public schools where it is impossible to gauge the physical and mental alertness of the youngster, his fatigue, etc. Yet the IQ scores are stored in the files of many bureaucracies and are made available to teachers, counselors, social workers, probation officers, the police, and practically anyone else (except the child and his family) who wants quickly to pigeonhole a person, perhaps for life.

To digress from Victoria for a moment, two of the very first cases which Lew and I worked on in 1970 underlined some of the problems with IQ scores.

Diane Martin had been in the Audy Home for nine months on a neglect and MINS petition when we were appointed to represent her. The DCFS was attempting to place her at Lincoln but claimed that since it was overcrowded there, it would take an additional four or five months to get her in. The Juvenile Court judge had us get involved because he hoped we could pressure the DCFS into getting her into Lincoln earlier.

Diane came from a very poor family—twelve children and two parents sharing a three-room apartment in one of the city's worst slums. She had become pregnant by one of her brothers when she was twelve, and had been in the Audy Home for five months before her child was born and for four months afterward. When I talked to her, she spoke with intelligence and insight about her background, problems, and hopes for the future—even about politics. There was no doubt in my mind that the IQ score was grossly in error. Then one day, when I gave Diane some legal papers to read and sign, I noticed that she held them within several inches of her face. I told her she would ruin her eyes by reading in that fashion, and she replied that she was blind in one eye and had poor vision in the other. Apparently, she had once had glasses, but they had been broken. She had not had a pair during her entire stay in the Audy Home, and could not remember if she had worn them while being tested in the schools. We presented these facts to the Juvenile Court and had Diane talk to the judge. The DCFS continued to insist she was retarded, although they did admit that the caseworker assigned to Diane had never spoken to her. The Court ordered Diane placed in a foster home.

Tammy Larsen was an even sadder case—an eleven-year-old girl who had been in the Audy Home for almost a year when we were appointed to represent her. She had been deaf and dumb from birth and had never gone to school, indeed had seldom been outside her mother's housing-project apartment. Now the DCFS conducts a school for the deaf and dumb in a downstate Illinois community, and there have been many allegations throughout the years that this school discriminated against Chicagoans, especially if they were black. Tammy was brought to the school for testing, to determine if she should be placed there.

After several hours, the tester reported that she was "hopelessly retarded." I asked a Chicago psychiatrist if one could test a deaf and dumb girl with Tammy's background in several hours, and he answered that it would be impossible to test even a deaf and dumb child from a *normal* background in less than several days. However, basing their decision on those tests, the DCFS evidently determined that it would just as soon have Tammy vegetate. Luckily, we were able to pressure it—in a lawsuit and by leaking the facts to the press—to send Tammy to an excellent school for the deaf on the West Coast. Two years later, she was able to read and to express herself in sign language.

Cases like Tammy's and Diane's had hardened us. By 1973, we were very leery of the facts on file about Victoria Murray. And it seemed more and more important, if children were to be kept out of the places where the state dumped them, to assure that they would not be pigeonholed either temporarily or forever. Just as important as an adequate screening and a hearing, was the need to keep out of the files all the useless hearsay, the all too often unfounded and untrue claptrap about people's so-called emotional and intellectual lives. The "psychosocial" statements in the children's files were normally prepared by people with no training, and they often condemned children for life. We did not trust even the "psychosocials" prepared by experts. Prejudicial statements about how such-and-such a child is autocratic, sexually promiscuous, frigid, retarded, disturbed, hysterical, violent, a toughie, obnoxious, etc., clutter these "expert" records. We thought it was junk. We were fed up with having it in the kids' files. So, together with ruling on the question of having an adequate screening process when a youngster was put in an institution for the retarded, we asked Judge Schneider also to consider formulating rules to safeguard what could be placed in a child's file. Victoria had been brought back from Missouri by the DCFS pursuant to our demands, and we put her on the stand to testify.

The social workers and newspaper reporters who half-filled the courtroom were prepared to hear the incoherent babbling of a semi-idiot who might have to be restrained because of her violence. But Victoria—a slight, attractive, black seventeen-year-old—testified with the utmost clarity, in her firm, clipped, Jamaican accent. As her story unfolded, the courtroom became hushed, Judge Schneider sat with his head between his hands, shaking it from side to side.

Victoria testified that she had come from Jamaica with her mother, who was a domestic in one of the fashionable suburbs on Chicago's North Shore. The girl lived with her mother for a month or two before being hired out as a domestic herself. In an eighteen-month period of time, she had worked as a maid and baby sitter in four different suburban homes—paid at varying rates but always provided with food and board. Finally, one of the families suggested that she enroll herself in New Trier High School in Winnetka, which she did. She started at New Trier in the fall of 1971 and continued to live and work as a domestic and baby sitter. However, her counselor thought that this was too rigorous a schedule for a fifteen-year-old adolescent, and called the DCFS, hoping that it could get Victoria into a foster home.

The DCFS caseworker met with Victoria at New Trier and told her she was going to be placed in a foster home on Chicago's South Side. Victoria, whose only experience of America had been in Winnetka, was frightened and told the caseworker that she did not want to live on the South Side because she had heard it was a violent area. But apparently, the caseworker felt that since Victoria was black she belonged there.

During the meeting, Victoria struggled with the caseworker and ran off, took the train to Chicago, and stayed with a friend overnight. In the meantime, the caseworker went to the home where Victoria was living and removed her clothes. The next day, Victoria discovered what had happened and went to the DCFS office to get her belongings. When she arrived, she struggled with the officials and was charged with aggravated battery. She was placed in the Audy Home from which, five days later, she was committed to Elgin State Mental Hospital. Victoria remained at Elgin for several months before being sent by the DCFS to the Missouri facility.

She testified that there were about seventy-five youngsters at the institution, and all but a few were severely retarded. "They couldn't do anything for themselves. They couldn't go to the bathroom. Somebody had to dress them. And there was this one boy there; he just would blow up, and he can hurt people and stuff like that."

Victoria testified that she was forced to take tranquilizing drugs which made her sleepy, and that if she refused to take them, they were given to her by injection. She also testified about medication given to her:

Q: Now, besides [the tranquilizing drugs] did they give you —force you to take any other drug or pill?

A: Just birth control.

Q: Did you want to take birth-control pills?

A: No, so they started giving it in shots.

Q: Did you tell them you didn't want to take it?

A: Yes.

Q: And what did they do to you when you took them?

A: (No response.)

Q: Did it hurt your body at all?

A: Yes.

Q: Did you argue with them and tell them there was no reason for you to take birth-control pills?

A: Yes, but they said it's to regulate our period so we just had to take it.

Q: Now, I don't want to embarrass you. Was there any reason you felt in your own mind you should be forced to take the pills or shots?

A: No.

We later learned that the shots given to Victoria and other youngsters was a drug which had not yet been medically approved by the FDA but which had showed in certain tests administered on dogs to be carcinogenic by the FDA. When a Chicago journalist questioned a DCFS medical adviser concerning this drug, he responded, "You have to test drugs on somebody, and Illinois girls are as good as anybody else." The poor man was fired within forty-eight hours, of course, but more for his lack of diplomacy, one suspects, than for his views on experimentation with children.

Victoria testified that she was given two jobs in Missouri and paid $6 a week for her work. Six mornings a week she cleaned the bathrooms and five days a week she worked with a group of eighteen retarded children, teaching them to talk, play games, and work with puzzles. Although she was supposed to be a teacher's aide, apparently the teacher had left and for at least part of the time Victoria was in charge by herself.

Within the week following Victoria's testimony, the DCFS removed twelve of the fourteen remaining Illinois youngsters at the Missouri institution. Of course, they claimed they were going to bring them back anyway. However, Victoria's testimony had even more far-reaching effects. Originally Dr. Miller and the DCFS bureaucracy had refused to cooperate with the DMH in formulating a screening process. But shortly after her testimony and the surrounding (somewhat sensational) media coverage of it, the DCFS agreed to allow all of its wards to be screened by a DMH committee before being committed to any public or private psychiatric facility.

To what extent the trivia cluttering up the children's files should be screened was a more complex question, and we agreed to negotiate with the DCFS in an attempt to reach a reasonable settlement. Of course, even with the good intentions of their new chief counsel, reaching a solution was extremely difficult. The entire juvenile-justice system is a limitless wasteland of insanity. Attempting to straighten out the irrelevant nonsense that went into the files was like going into the middle of a gigantic swamp and trying to build a small but firm island, having no way to get on or off it. Not only would it be impossible to build such an island but it would be virtually useless once it was constructed.

10

The Family-Saving Quagmire

INSTEAD OF enjoying the sands and sights along Lake Michigan during the bright, hot summer of 1973, we were involved in major litigation against the Departments of Children and Family Services and Mental Health before Judges Schneider and White. We wore down a triangular path between our noise-conditioned office, the Civic Center, where Judge Schneider sat, and the Juvenile Court, where Judge White heard cases. Everything that I have described in the last chapter was going on at once. Before Judge White, we were either preparing for a hearing or trying cases that challenged the adequacy of treatment given to neglected children by the DCFS, the adequacy of placement of Illinois children in Texas institutions, and Denise Wade's hysterectomy. At the same time, before Judge Schneider, we were litigating the adequacy of treatment of youngsters in psychiatric hospitals, the need to have screening devices for youngsters put in facilities for the retarded, and the issues surrounding the files. Stories about these cases, particularly those of Victoria Murray, Diane Martin, and the Texas institutions, were constantly in and out of the newspapers. Of course, this is precisely what we wanted. The more the public was informed about the juvenile justice system, the more we hoped they would question it.

In early August, all five Chicago daily newspapers were running articles concerning the 500 kids in Texas, and were more and more critical of the DCFS. Because of the heightened public awareness and the outcry in the news media, we thought it would be propitious to file two more lawsuits several months ahead of our original schedule. The first was designed to reopen the Audy Home case before Judge Philip Tone in federal court. We had noticed that during the late spring and early summer the DCFS population had risen significantly in the Audy Home—by mid-July, there were forty-five DCFS children incarcerated there, which was almost one fourth of its population—and the DCFS had broken the agreement on numerous occasions we had made with them in order to dismiss the suit before Judge Tone. The DCFS caseworkers were not visiting the wards in Audy, and their supervisors were not coming to court to explain why the children were kept there. So, by early August, we had four major lawsuits going against the DCFS simultaneously, each either in the hearing stage or heading for it.

The DCFS we now confronted was in many ways not quite the same as the one we had first done battle with in 1970. In early 1973, Dr. Jerome Miller had been appointed by the governor as the Director of the DCFS. Dr. Miller had previously headed up the Youth Commission in Massachusetts and had been the center of much controversy there when he closed down most of the penal institutions for youth in that state. When he came to Illinois, he tried to revise and reform the DCFS, but the entrenched bureaucracy made it harder for him to make headway. Initially, we had good relationships with Dr. Miller, but as the tempo of our litigation increased in the summer of 1973, the cordiality broke down. Still, we thought he was doing an excellent job and was being unjustly criticized: it was not his fault that there were over 500 Illinois kids in Texas, 200 and more in mental hospitals, and scores in institutions for the retarded and the Audy Home, nor was it his fault that as he moved to lessen the DCFS population in any one of these dumping grounds, it automatically rose in the others. In part to get Dr. Miller off the hook and in part to take advantage of the media coverage of the juvenile justice system, we prematurely filed one of our most important lawsuits in August.

Most of the neglected children with whom I had been concerned—and whom I have described in this book—were initially wards of the Juvenile Court. But the Court immediately gives over guardianship to the DCFS and serves as no more than a rubber stamp for DCFS decisions. The result is that the DCFS, one of Illinois' richest agencies, had an exceedingly broad mandate to engage in "child-saving," with virtually limitless discretion to evaluate, direct, channel, place, "treat," and, finally, expel those children under its care. However, because its case load was so great, the DCFS subordinated its duty of treatment and care to the practical requirements of efficiency. The result was, as Judge Schneider commented, that children under the guardianship of the state all too often suffered a kind of neglect which the law would not have countenanced had it occurred in their own homes.

In fact—as I have perhaps already made clear in the case histories recounted here—the DCFS really provided almost no services at all. Only a tiny part of its vast bureaucracy actually had anything to do with taking care of children. In a sense, the DCFS was merely a giant referral agency, relying upon licensed foster homes and private child-care facilities to cope with the "parentage" duties imposed by the law upon the state. Since there were many more children to be placed than there were openings within the private child-care system, and since the DCFS did not maintain or supervise placements of its own wards, it was unfortunately in the position of being forced to accept whatever was available in the market place, irrespective of the needs of many of the children it was mandated to serve.

Traditionally, then, in Illinois as in most other states, the people who ran the private child-care facilities dictated to the state exactly how it was to conduct its child-saving system. Certainly, in Illinois, the private agencies, through their associations, were the piper playing the tune to which the state all too willingly danced. This has meant that the development of state programs for delivery of services to families has been blocked, and the state prevented from maintaining its own institutional placements.

After three years of litigating within the juvenile justice system and investigating it thoroughly (and particularly because of the watchdog job assigned to us by Judge Schneider) we came to the considered opinion that the private child-care associations were even more to blame for many of the horrors than the state bureaucracy itself—which was hardly guiltless. While dictating to the state and the DCFS how they were to conduct their business and forcing their own facilities on the state agencies, these associations—which thrived on their monopoly and yet were not really viable without state financial assistance—through their selection system, forced black and brown children and white children with behavioral problems into the various dumping grounds. Practically all the private institutions maintained racial quotas, accepting no more than a certain percentage of black and brown youngsters. The most enlightened ones seem to have a roughly 60–40 white-to-minority population; many would only accept one or two black or brown children. Most of them rejected *any* child, white or black, if he had real problems that required attention. Girls who were sexually promiscuous and boys who were openly defiant were never accepted by the system. Moreover, the institutions relied heavily on IQ tests in ferreting out any child who appeared to be less than of average intelligence. Lastly, if a child living at one of these facilities developed a behavioral problem, even if he had been there for years, he would be quickly traded into the system for a new youngster. Traditionally, the DCFS readily allowed this type of trade to occur.

The result was that the children who needed help the least got the best care, while the ones who needed it most often ended up in mental hospitals, the Audy detention center, or the Texas places. Ironically, only the Texas institutions were expensive for the DCFS: the Audy Home and the mental-health system cost it nothing, and the private agencies charged the state anywhere from $14 to over $40 per day per child for their custody.

While over half of the DCFS wards from Cook County were black or brown, only a handful of these trickled into the private system. It came as no surprise to be told by James Jordan, for twenty years the Director of the Audy Home, that more than 60 per cent of all DCFS wards in *his* institution were from minority backgrounds. And in our suit against the DMH, we were able to judge that about 60 per cent of the DCFS wards in mental-health facilities were black or brown. In the Lincoln School for the Retarded, 90 per cent of the kids were black, and of the ten children who did not belong there nine were black; in the two apparently most punitive institutions in Texas most of the DCFS wards were black. It was harder to tell how many of the white children in these places exhibited mere behavioral problems—that is, how many white kids were incarcerated even though they needed no psychiatric care and were not retarded. But as the tempo of our lawsuits against the DCFS picked up, and as Dr. Miller came under increasing fire, both from the press and from his own staff, the private agencies smugly jumped in and also attacked him, pointing out how successful they were in treating children in their institutions. Of course, their success ratio was quite high, since they accepted no problem youngsters and immediately rejected any who became so. It was difficult to know how many of these "problems" Dr. Miller actually had on his hands.

The lawsuit we filed prematurely, at least in part to help Dr. Miller, ironically named him as well as the state as the defendants. In the suit, we asked the Juvenile Court to order the DCFS and the state to stop assigning children to private facilities if they used racial quotas, and we listed eighteen of the wealthiest places and cited the numbers of black, white, and brown children in each. Although the suit was directed nominally against the state, the real defendants were the child-care agencies.

Needless to say, the case was a bombshell that infuriated many professionals in the child-saving business in Illinois. As we gradually proceeded toward a hearing on the issues, strangely enough, the private agencies began to accept more minority youngsters.

WHILE WE were banging away at the treatment given neglected children in the traditional system of private versus public welfare services, we attacked, through the appellate process, what we considered to be the overbroad jurisdiction of the Juvenile Court over so-called neglected children and parents.

Since the juvenile justice system was organized a century ago, the prevailing philosophy under which it has operated considers that separation of youngsters from environments "injurious to his or her welfare" is often necessary to save the child. In the nineteenth century, this separation was done in John Calvin's name. Today, it is accomplished in Sigmund Freud's.

According to the neglect (in some states, "dependency") statutes, children are neglected if they live in an environment that is injurious to their welfare, or if their own behavior is injurious to their welfare. If the court finds that either of these two situations exists, then a finding of neglect can be entered, the child is made a ward of the Juvenile Court, and the Court appoints a state welfare agency as guardian. Although in Illinois and in several other states, parents who need government assistance for their children may voluntarily give up custodianship to the state for a temporary period, federal guidelines compel parents on public assistance to admit to neglect in court before the help can be gotten.

The Assistant Public Defender, who represented most parents in neglect court in Cook County, and our office, which represented some, together estimated that in 1971 only about 5 per cent of the several thousand neglect cases involved physical abuse. About 90 per cent of the cases heard by the same court were there for reasons almost solely related to poverty. But even under the dire circumstances in which many of these children were raised, it is doubtful that they were really *neglected.* Certainly, they were not raised in the style of the middle-class caseworkers investigating them; besides, they were the victims not only of grinding poverty but of bad housing, racial discrimination, and the worst schools in the city. Many, if not most, of the children being herded through the neglect court did legitimately need help, and so did their families. But should the help have been to take the kids away from their families and put them in orphanages or the houses of strangers? Sometimes they turned up in neglect court because their parents were going through some emotional and/or physical illness and temporarily could not care for them. Sometimes the child himself (as in the case of Matilda McIntosh) was encountering emotional, educational, or other difficulties and needed some type of expert assistance which the family could not afford. What happens to children caught up in the juvenile quagmire I have detailed already, but a few examples of *parents* who were compelled to give guardianship to the state is perhaps in order.

Monica Voigt was a very intelligent black woman with the face and figure of a fashion model. She had been raised in a middle-class neighborhood, finished school and married when she was seventeen. Within a year she had a child and her husband walked out on her. Within the next several years, she was disowned by her parents, had two more children out of wedlock, and was living on the near South Side in a slum neighborhood with all her children. Monica woke up at the age of twenty-six—as many women do in the same situation—with three children, living in one of the most impoverished and crime-ridden areas of the country, in a welfare syndrome which did not allow her simultaneously to get a job and raise her children, and seeing only continued and increasing degradation for herself and her children. She came very close to a nervous breakdown, and was actually placed in a mental hospital for a few days, during which time welfare workers took her children and put them in two separate foster homes. After her release from the mental hospital, Monica determined that the only way to escape the vicious circle she was trapped in was to leave her children in the foster homes for a while, get a job, go off welfare, and maybe even work toward some college credits. Perhaps in a year or two she would be in a position to take her children back and offer them a better life, as well as lead a more fulfilling one herself. Since she was on welfare, she was not allowed simply to give her children up voluntarily for state guardianship, but had to go to Juvenile Court and admit that she had "neglected" them. Once she had done this, the children were placed with strangers, who received about $130 per month per child to care for them. (Monica, who had been getting about $40 per child, went about trying to straighten her life out, but if she had gotten the same kind of money the foster parents got, she would never have given the children up.)

Karen Greene was a middle-aged, slightly unstable, and physically ill woman with two children, thirteen and eight years old. She had been divorced from her husband for about five years. According to the school social worker, the thirteen-year-old boy was developing emotional problems, and although he ranked first in his eighth-grade class, the other boys taunted and picked on him for his slight build and because of his somewhat eccentric mother. The mother had a bronchial condition which caused her periodically to be hospitalized, and a social worker talked Mrs. Greene into giving the DCFS custody so that the boy could go to a boarding school and receive counseling until Mrs. Greene could get back on her feet. From what I read in the DCFS report, it seems very probable that the boy's "problems" could have been resolved more cheaply outside of a private school. Since his mother was not on welfare, she did not have to admit to "neglect," and was able to voluntarily place the boy with the DCFS. Aaron was then sent to a Roman Catholic orphanage, where on occasion he had to attend Mass. Mrs. Greene, who was a religious Orthodox Jew, complained to the DCFS, and he was transferred to a Jewish foster home.

Mrs. Greene often and bitterly questioned the DCFS caseworkers as to why she had had to give the child to the state in order that he could receive therapy, when he was not given *any* therapy either at the orphanage or with the foster parents. Caseworkers hate "bitches." Needless to say, they despised Mrs. Greene. The boy's bar mitzvah came while he was with the foster parents, and, although they did have a ceremony for him, they allowed only Mrs. Greene and one or two close family friends to attend. Again the mother complained. Shortly thereafter, the foster parents asked the agency to take Aaron away because of the mother's "constant interference." Back to an orphanage, this time a Protestant one (where, according to Mrs. Greene, he was the only Jewish boy), again he received no help for his alleged instability. The caseworkers from the agency told the mother that in order for her son to receive therapy she would have to go to court and admit to "neglect." By this time Mrs. Greene had not had any guardianship over her son of any kind for over six months, but she went through the ghastly process, still hoping that Aaron could be aided.

At this point the orphanage and the DCFS had Mrs. Greene in a corner. They cut her visitation rights to one a month and sometimes would not even allow her that one occasion. When she did visit Aaron, she was forced to see him in the presence of the social worker. When she demanded that her son be returned to her, the DCFS argued that if she wanted her son she would have to go back to court, file a motion to "vacate the neglect," and prove to the court that she was no longer a neglectful mother. This predictably drove Mrs. Greene into hysterics. In vain she tried to explain to the caseworker that she had not in fact neglected her child; after all, she had been convinced by the *very same caseworker* that admitting to "neglect" in order to give her child aid was exactly what a good mother would do.

What makes the situation even more complex for Mrs. Greene —and for most parents like her charged with emotional and environmental neglect—is that it is almost impossible to win such a lawsuit. The statute reads that any child is neglected who lives in an atmosphere, or whose behavior is, injurious to his or her behavior. In some sections of Chicago, practically every child growing up there could be so described. And with psychiatric testimony, it is not hard to show that just about any child's behavior is injurious to his welfare. The statute is one of those broad nets of legislation that catch every fish swimming through and allow the fisherman to choose which he wants to keep and which to throw back. Social agencies proposed it and social agencies love it.

The "neglect" statute is very similar to vagrancy statutes, many of which were recently struck down by the Supreme Court. These statutes generally say that people found loitering, walking the streets, and carrying on forms of unproductive enterprise may be arrested, prosecuted, and jailed. The Supreme Court struck down one such statute as violating the due-process clause, because "a statute which either forbids or requires the doing of an act in terms so vague that men of common intelligence must necessarily guess at its meaning and differ as to its application, violate the first essential of due process." As Mr. Justice Douglas pointed out in the 1972 case of *Papachristou* v. *Jacksonville,* since the statute covers practically every citizen, it gives the police the discretion to prosecute whom they wish. "Those generally implicated by the imprecise terms of the ordinance—poor people, nonconformists, dissenters, idlers—may be required to comport themselves according to the life-style deemed appropriate by the Jacksonville Police and the court." So, too, the poor, the dissenters, and nonconformists are often compelled to comport themselves and their family lives in the style dictated by private and public social-welfare agencies who attempt to "save" them, or else must face prosecution under vague, nebulous, and over-reaching statutes.

If two children are born at precisely the same moment and with potentially the same abilities, talents, drives, intelligence, and other substantial and accidental qualities needed to "succeed," but one is born in the Robert Taylor Homes on Chicago's South Side, and the other in Lake Forest, along Chicago's elite North Shore, quite obviously the only moment at which the two are equal is at the moment of conception. From that point forward, the gap of inequality widens, and by the time the child reaches adolescence it is a chasm. Family, neighborhood, milieu, friends, travel, schools, and a hundred other influences work to separate the two children into two different worlds—whether actual or potential.

If, in fact, a child needs help, why must his parents be forced to go through the degrading process of admitting to "neglect" in order to get it from the state? Indeed, since it is in part at least state practices (for instance, the educational system) that force failure upon some and allow success for others, why should not the state provide assistance free of judicial labels when a child needs it? Why should a parent have to go to court, or be forced to accept advice from a middle-class "expert" whose only expertise is a college degree and the luck that he did not grow up in a slum? Who is getting the most out of these conferences: the poor person who by undergoing a session with a do-gooder receives some type of benefit for his child, or the caseworker who receives some type of emotional uplift by doing good?

Often, parents admit to "neglect" or seek state assistance for reasons closely related to a simple lack of adequate finances. The family may have been on welfare and receiving $30–$40 a month per child. The child is taken from them and put in a home where the stranger who becomes the foster parent gets about $130 (plus other medical and clothing allowances) for the same purpose.

Institutions that purportedly provide not only care, but some form of "therapy," get anywhere from $15 to $40 *a day* for a child. Yet what benefits do these places provide? Recently one of the "better" institutions in Illinois admitted that its $35-a-day program could not provide therapy for the youngsters whom the DCFS wanted to place there—kids with emotional problems but not so disturbed as to require psychiatric hospitalization. So the Agency asked for, and got, $70 per day per child from the state of Illinois. When I found out that it was sending one of my clients to that institution, I not so facetiously suggested that it give the $25,000 (the cost for one child per year) to the parents and let them move out of their old neighborhood, buy a new home, or send the girl to a good private school. Perhaps everyone would have been happier.

IN 1973, our office filed two lawsuits, one in the state and the other in the federal court, seeking to overturn the broad neglect statute and the regulation forcing welfare mothers to admit to "neglect" in order to receive state assistance for their children. The case attacking the neglect statute is now pending in the Illinois Supreme Court. The second issue, inextricably intertwined with the vague neglect statute—the equal-protection issue of whether the state could compel welfare mothers to admit to "neglect" while accepting voluntary placement of children from parents who were not on welfare—was the object of our civil-rights complaint filed in federal court, asking that this regulation be declared unconstitutional.

After several months of negotiation, the DCFS agreed to revise its regulations to allow welfare parents to place their children voluntarily with the agency when assistance was needed. It even agreed to inform all parents of this right—including the cases which the DCFS believed could legitimately be described as true child neglect—so that it could negotiate with the Juvenile Court through a lawyer and perhaps arrive at a compromise.

But the problem here, as with the nebulous neglect statute, is whether legislatures and the American people are willing to move away from the nineteenth-century idea of focusing blame on a parent for the problems of their children. The problems the children have are no different than those the parents had before them and, more often than not, are a direct result of them. And the parents are not wholly to blame—especially when they too are at the mercy of poverty, unemployment, racial discrimination, and a variety of other identifiable phenomena.

The cost of the present juvenile justice and welfare system is great not only in terms of the loss of dignity which the people who rely upon it must suffer but also in terms of the dollars and cents the American taxpayers must fork over. The incredible history of one Lottie Ervin offers a good example of this dual outrage.

Mrs. Ervin had four children when her husband left her in 1970. She was on welfare and received state funds under the "aid to dependent children" program when she and several other welfare mothers moved into an abandoned church in Chicago's West Side after being unable to find adequate alternative housing; since no one else was using the church, they said, they might as well. Naturally, the authorities did not concur. Still, it was eventually agreed that they could stay on, and they lived in the church for the next two and a half years, until the building was sold to some developers who wanted to demolish it. The developers were willing to give the families time to move out, and by December 1972 all but Mrs. Ervin and her children had found homes. On the night of December 17, 1972, four police officers showed up at Mrs. Ervin's door. They told her there had been complaints that she was not properly feeding her children. (By this time, Mrs. Ervin had another child, then three months old, by her ex-husband.) The policemen searched the cupboards and refrigerator to see how much food she had. They told her that there was not enough and that they would have to take the children to the police station in order to feed them. (The children ranged in age from fourteen to three months. Each was bright, none was underweight, and all had adequate wardrobes.)

Mrs. Ervin was naturally horrified, and in her anger struck one of the officers. She was subdued and placed in the paddy wagon, and she and her children were taken to the local police district, where she remained in the wagon for an hour until the police came and got her. They then told her she was under arrest for battery and that her children would be put in foster homes. She was charged with child neglect and with battery.

On the next morning, friends bonded her out, and she began to look for her children. In the meantime, while she was at the Cook County Jail and being processed through the criminal court, her children had been taken to Juvenile Court where a DCFS social worker told the judge that they had been neglected by their mother, presently in jail. The judge gave temporary custody to the DCFS and continued the case until the end of January. With the help of a local church group, Mrs. Ervin was able to discover that her children were in the custody of the DCFS, but this took several frantic days.

Representatives of the DCFS told Mrs. Ervin and the church worker when the new court date would be and that she had a right to contest it. Until then, she neither knew where her children actually were nor was told she had a right to visit them.

In early January, Mrs. Ervin was visited by the church worker, who told her that the three-month-old child, Cindy, had died in her foster home. Apparently, she had been inadvertently placed in a bathtub full of scalding water, and the shock had killed her almost instantly. Shortly thereafter, Mrs. Ervin came to our office.

Now at one time Mrs. Ervin had been a very militant welfare mother, but when I first met her in January 1973, she was completely acceptant of the state's will. She hardly questioned the fact that her children were in foster homes and that her daughter had died. Her only complaint was that a son was still in the same foster home where her daughter had died and that the agency refused to remove him. We called and wrote the Director of Chicago operations of the DCFS but were told both orally and in writing that the child would be taken out within two months anyway, since it was a "temporary foster home." When I got the letter, I phoned the Director and told him he had twenty-four hours to take the boy out or face a federal civil-rights suit. Within sixteen hours, the child had been switched to a different foster home; in a month, the DCFS returned all the children to Mrs. Ervin and, several months thereafter, dismissed all neglect charges against her. We defended Mrs. Ervin in the criminal case and she was found not guilty of the charges of assault on the police officer or of neglect of her children before the jury, but she was convicted of resisting arrest. The judge, however, after entering a finding on the verdict refused to sentence her. We are now working on a wrongful death action against the state because of the child's death.

Mrs. Ervin's trip through the do-good bureaucracy of Illinois during the Christmas-New Year holiday season will serve as a good example of, among other things, the tremendous cost of our present system. Consider the salaries paid to the four police officers on that night in December, along with their three appearances in Juvenile Court and a three-day jury trial in criminal court, the concomitant cost of clerks, bailiffs, court reporters, two judges, prosecuting attorneys, and our own office staff; all of this is paid from public funds. We are probably talking in terms of $7000 or $8000 for the activities of a few days on this one case. If we include the cost of the foster homes for four children for two months at $140 per home, the salaries of the social workers and the secretaries, the cost of the paper work, and the funeral, we are bringing in another $3000. Assuming that Mrs. Ervin did not have enough food in her house on December 17, then the simplest solution might have been to buy her additional food at a possible cost of $25 or $30. Instead, the state of Illinois paid out or will pay in the neighborhood of $10,000 so that it can attempt to assess guilt for the poverty and need from which Mrs. Ervin suffered. And we have not even begun to talk about the indignities she endured, the anxieties, the disruption in her children's lives as they were separated and cast out among strangers. And, lastly, how does one assess dollars and cents to pay for the lost baby's life?

11

Looking Back and Looking Forward

DURING our first three years in the Legal Aid office, we cut down our work load and represented fewer clients, hoping thereby to have a greater impact upon the juvenile justice system and make it work more efficiently and benignly for the youngsters and families ensnared in it. For those clients whom we did represent, we tried to do everything possible for them both during the litigations and afterwards. Some clients, like Bobby Crane and Matilda McIntosh, were represented over many years and cases. The litigation helped some of our clients and gave them hope for a brighter future. But for others, although the cases we brought on their behalf may have wrought major changes in the law, they themselves were unaffected and continued on their downward slide to poverty and crime.

Cathy Beesley and Elenor Miromir are good examples of children who were completely unaffected by our lawsuits. Both of these youngsters were jailed as minors in need of supervision, and both remained in the Department of Corrections for about a year. After release, Elenor got a high-school diploma and went to college a while before dropping out and leaving Chicago. Cathy returned to her West Side ghetto home. She still does not get along well with her mother, but seems doomed to follow her into poverty and welfare: no doubt she will then cycle this syndrome on to her own children. Although the juvenile justice system did no actual harm to these two girls, neither did it benefit them in the slightest. It cubbyholed them physically and pigeonholed them as delinquents.

Karen Greene, the Jewish mother whose child ended up in Christian orphanages, is another example of a person caught within the web of the system who got out early enough to be relatively unhurt. After we sued the DCFS on her behalf, it agreed to give her temporary custody of her son. Shortly after, she called me to report that she was about to leave for New Mexico. She apologized, but said she was tired of being pushed around by the state of Illinois. I did my duty to the canons of ethics and told her that leaving the state was technically illegal. She asked me if I were really serious, and I remained judiciously silent. Then she asked me if I had any advice for her before she left. The last words I spoke with her were to advise her not to seek the help of the state of New Mexico if her son had any adolescent problems.

Of the four boys we represented in the federal aspects of the Sheridan case, only John Topps—the runaway who spent nine consecutive months in solitary—seems headed for better things. After we pleaded him guilty in the criminal court of LaSalle County, he spent five months at the Illinois State Penitentiary. Since Topps had no high-school diploma and was an ex-con, it was hard for him to find a job, but despite this and despite the constant pressures of his neighborhood, he stayed straight and finally found several menial jobs, as a janitor at a night club and later as a short-order cook. Finally, he got a relatively good job as a laborer for a construction company and started attending night school. He still has a long way to go at nineteen, but with a little luck and a lot of hard work, he may make it—one of the few youngsters whom we have represented to whom we could give this prophecy.

The three other boys in the case did not come out so well. Within a year, two were back in criminal court on very serious charges. One of the greatest letdowns I have ever had was picking up a copy of the *Chicago Sun-Times* and reading an article captioned, FIVE YOUTHS, 17, CHARGED IN SOUTH SIDE RAPE CASE. One of them was Larry Woodson.

Matilda McIntosh was finally released from Geneva after almost three years. She was "placed on independent living" at the age of sixteen by the DCFS. This meant simply that the DCFS would take care of her room and board each month, and it was also supposed to try to help find her a job or to help her in her further education. However, it was not doing much of anything, probably because the $500,000 lawsuit against DCFS in her case was proceeding to trial.

We were finally able to force the DCFS to provide at least adequate custody for Joe Todd, the orphan whom we had represented through two Audy Home lawsuits and who had been chained to his bed in Texas for killing a dog. But before it did, it managed to have him committed to the Department of Corrections. The DCFS had been trying to do this for some time, because it felt they had run out of "placement possibilities." The bogus crime for which he finally was charged was attacking a two-hundred and twenty pound guard at the Audy Home. While I was gone from Chicago on a brief holiday in early 1973, they raced into Juvenile Court, claimed that Todd was delinquent because he had not only attacked the guard but had since run away several times. The caseworker asked the Court to commit Joe to the DOC. This suggestion was followed by the judge, and in February 1973 Todd was incarcerated. Within six weeks, we had the commitment vacated, but not until we had threatened to bring the DCFS back to federal court and to embarrass it in every conceivable legal way. Joe was put into a foster home of a middle-aged electrician, where he is doing quite well.

Bobby Crane was one of our greatest problems. We had gotten

Bobby released from the Audy Home, and from Chester; he then went to a foster home on Chicago's near South Side and was given an allowance of $10 a week. However, he continued to get into scrape after scrape. He was arrested on several occasions for stealing cars. Normally, he would either drive out to Elgin State Hospital or just drive for hour after lonely hour each morning, back and forth over some stark, deserted street. With the assistance of sympathetic prosecutors we were able to keep him out of serious trouble. However, for several months he did learn about yet another institution—the Cook County prison.

After several conferences and with the assistance of Judge Schneider, DCFS officials agreed that because of what the State had done in "behavioralizing" Bobby into being a thoroughly helpless and dependent person they would now try, whatever the cost, to help him to help himself. His case was assigned to one of their best and most dedicated caseworkers, Roland Julla. Bob was put in a small hotel where Roland could keep an eye on him and give him a small daily allowance. Lastly, a psychiatrist whom Bobby respected was retained. However, since Bobby was quickly approaching his twenty-first birthday the officials pointed out that they could no longer be responsible for him by law. We then filed a petition before Judge White asking him to consider Bobby nineteen, and argued that the state owed it to Bobby to try to get him on his feet. We pointed out that when Bobby was first picked up in 1960 he had been fortuitously given the age of seven, when the caseworker thought he might also be five. We then showed how this given age of seven caused psychologists to argue that Bobby was retarded and place him in an institution for the retarded. Finally, we pointed out that just about everyone now agreed that Bobby was not retarded—though he was institutionalized.

While the petition was pending, I took Bobby's enormous four-hundred-page file home with me—all the records from DCFS, DMH, Public Aid, and the Juvenile Court. It was thick with the usual claptrap and trivia. I divided the papers into several piles on my living-room floor and tried to cross-index them according to events and categories.

As I began to read the material I slowly put together a chilling puzzle. Apparently, Bobby had not been so fortuitously given his last name. His mother's name and town—a small one in Ohio—were known. Other pieces of evidence from his mother's past all pointed to one irrefutable conclusion. Bobby Crain was five—maybe even four—when he was picked up in Skid Row. A careless error by a caseworker combined with the fact that those who were responsible for his placement probably never saw him had caused Bobby to be cubbyholed as retarded. The motions that error set off in his files and within the state bureaucracies were to take their tragic toll.

Two psychiatrists who had previously examined him both stated that he was the most thoroughly institutionalized person they had ever seen. By the time he was twenty, he had been virtually "pavlovianized" by the state into becoming a dependent person. Although the state files on him suggested that Bobby was retarded, disturbed, and a bit of a criminal, he was none of these things. Well, I suppose in a sense one could say he was disturbed. He certainly was angry. He was angry because his mother had deserted him as a small child. He was angry with the state for jailing him at the Audy Home at the age of five and in a series of institutions for the retarded for the next four or five years. He was even angrier at the state and the Juvenile Court for putting him back in the Audy Home when he was twelve and thirteen. He was mad at the world for having put him in a mental home—Elgin—in the last years of his adolescence. And, lastly, he was angry because he had been sent to a prison for the criminally insane when he was neither a criminal nor insane.

And Bobby was retarded, too. No, he was not retarded in the sense of having a low-intelligence quotient. In fact, I believe he is quite bright. Nor is he retarded in the cultural sense. Years of watching television and seeing movies have taught Bobby much about our culture and the advantages which flow to the "successful." Bobby is retarded because he is different from the rest of us—different because of the years he has spent in institutions and because it has taught him that he must exist by manipulating, by whining, by begging, and by doing whatever else is necessary to get on in his narrowly circumscribed world.

When presented the evidence, Judge White did order Bobby's files to reflect his true age. However, this ruling and the stepped-up assistance for Bobby may have been fourteen years too late. He was arrested on several other occasions and though we continued to manage to keep him out of prison, his luck is running out. Bobby, in all probability, will never commit a violent crime. He is too gentle. But he is the sort of person who, by committing a series of minor thefts and other misdemeanors, will "do life" —a year at a time.

AFTER THREE years of trying to reform the bureaucracies of Illinois' juvenile justice system, we could look back with some justifiable pride on our accomplishments. When we began, Sheridan had well over 300 juvenile inmates, but three years and four lawsuits later, there were none. Three years previously, the Audy Home had almost 400 minors, of whom about a third were "neglected," but by 1973 there were only about 200 children in the Audy Home, of whom less than 25 were wards of the DCFS. The incarceration of runaways had decreased tremendously over the three years, and in 1972 the Illinois legislature enacted a law that outlawed it entirely by July 1973. The number of children not in need of mental-health care but placed in mental homes nevertheless was rapidly diminishing. New regulations we had forced on the DMH through our litigation greatly limited the use of punishments, drugs, and the institutionalization of youthful inmates in maximum-security jails. Moreover, the children under eighteen now had a right to a hearing.

And unwed fathers now had the right to contest their children's being taken from them, and the overbroad "neglect" statute was under attack. Having lost on the issue of whether children are entitled to be told of the consequences of a plea of guilty in family court and also to be told of their right to appeal in Illinois Supreme Court, we had successfully petitioned the federal court to determine the issue and, in October 1973, the state agreed to inform youths adequately of their rights. We were then also in the midst of proceedings determining the validity of the state's use of drugs on its wards and its screening and labeling procedures. We had exposed the "Texas connection" and were challenging what we believed to be a stacked deck against minority youngsters.

About the same time the U.S. Court of Appeals for the Seventh Circuit finally delivered decisions in the *McIntosh* and *Armstrong* cases. They reversed the District Court and remanded the cases for trial. In these precedent-setting opinions, the Seventh Circuit ruled that if we could prove our allegations about how restraints and other punishments were used by the DMH and DCFS, the constitutional rights of the children had been abused and the state would be liable for money damages. In concluding the *Armstrong* decision, the Court pointed out:

> . . . We doubt that the treatment alleged—tying children to their beds in spread-eagled fashion, placing them in an area where others congregate for seventy-seven and one half hours, and forcing them to scrub walls for long periods while barely clothed—can be described as either "usual," a practice commonly used in other places, or consistent with public opinion regarding it, "evolving standards of decency" in a humane society. We conclude that the Plaintiffs' allegations, if proved, do state punishment which is cruel and unusual under the Eighth Amendment, as applied to the states through the Fourteenth Amendment.

Not only were we apparently achieving legal successes but because of media interest the public was being educated to the truths about what happens when a child becomes a ward of the state—that this did not mean a benign future for him, but all too often guaranteed the opposite. From all quarters the system was being questioned.

Still, when we detached ourselves and tried for that objectivity which allows one to see the forest instead of the trees, we had the kind of desperate feeling that Canute may have had when he tried to order the sea to recede. There had been change and movement; our lawsuits helped to expose areas of abuse and lent credence to a popular academic point of view that the problem with the juvenile-justice system is not that it has been tried and found wanting but that it has never been tried; we were often congratulated on our lawsuits by professionals for exposing the portions of the juvenile justice system which needed reform. To a certain degree, we did make an unequal, outmoded, never-really-functioning system operate more smoothly, and, hence, we not only prolonged it but gave it the aura of workability.

Those most intimately involved with juvenile and child welfare systems over the past decades have argued that all that was needed to make the system work was more money. But our feeling—even after all these successful lawsuits—was that we could pour the same amount of money into this system that we now pour into defense and still have little to show for it as long as the system remained the same. A judicial system, juvenile, criminal, or civil, is meant to resolve disputes between claimants which cannot be resolved out of court, and to punish those individuals who somehow upset society's balance. Trying to make a court become a rehabilitative social instrument has been a noble experiment, but nevertheless a failure.

In simpler times, when a person or family became involved in financial or other difficulties, his family, extended family, or subtribe was expected to help him and usually did. In modern, urbanized societies, we have not yet determined the way to get existing resources to those who actually need them without the intervening bureaucratic maze, which diverts so much of the money to its own uses and all too often forces the beneficiaries to grovel before middle-class bureaucrats. It is impossible to consider reform of the juvenile justice system without considering the reasons why this particular bureaucratic system of justice exists. Originially, the family court was the triumph of efforts made by social reformers who saw the children of immigrants—mostly Italians, Germans, and Irish—running around in the streets in unsupervised fashion. The parents often could not supervise these urchins because they were employed in nineteenth-century sweat shops, working long hours at low wages for the same families who produced the leading reformers attempting to save the children from their horrendous existence. Times have not changed. With the exception of that small percentage of youngsters legitimately charged with serious felony offenses, most of the children and families dragged before the court today are there for reasons closely related to racial attitudes and poverty. The court is expected to become some type of social instrument to resolve the problems that lack of money caused.

In Cook County, as elsewhere in America, the great majority of the children in juvenile court, the ones who end up under the guardianship of departments of children and family services, corrections, or mental health, come from the same inner-city and black neighborhoods. Most are poor. Many live in bleak, high-rise housing projects, and all of them attend the same type of schools. Many of their parents are on welfare. After condemning the children to live in segregated parts of town in deplorable circumstances, under a welfare system which degrades people, breaks up families, recycles the inherent problems from generation to generation, and compels these children to attend the worst conceivable schools, society then spends millions of dollars "rehabilitating" them. Then, when the millions spent in the juvenile justice system fail, we talk about pouring additional millions into it to somehow make the salvaging process better. If we should have learned anything from the War on Poverty, it is that pouring millions of dollars into programs which are allegedly intended for the poor, but which tend to assist middle-class bureaucrats and social workers, will be a failure. This is why I oppose a reform of the juvenile system by pouring more money into it and would favor doing away with the juvenile courts entirely, with the exception of the prosecution of older children who have committed serious felony offenses and parents who have physically abused children.

When the state's educational and public-assistance establishments do not resolve the problems caused by poverty (and indeed often compound them), and the problems are tossed into the juvenile-justice system, it is clear that we must look beyond the system itself in considering ways to reform it. Otherwise, we get into the same old game of dumping poor children and families from system to system and from one bureaucracy to another. Any attempt to reform a state bureaucracy that allegedly assists our poor citizens, without considering the effects upon the other bureaucracies and how to reform *them,* will be unsuccessful.

I do have several observations concerning reform of the juvenile justice system itself and reform of the haphazard ways by which we deliver services to poor, neglected, and delinquent youngsters. But these are merely observations and not solutions. No one could set out even a few solutions in several pages. Moreover, even if one had volumes to do it in, I still do not believe that one can successfully theorize about solutions to the problems outlined in this book. Others have tried—and much of what these authors have written about welfare, education, and court reforms should be considered and employed. Still, in the end, true reform can only occur in the trenches—where the poor, frustrated, undereducated, and powerless people whom I have tried to write about are caught, trapped by their own poverty and defenselessness on one hand, and by contradictory, ridiculous laws and incompetent bureaucrats on the other. It is far easier to theorize in books about how we will somehow make life better for these people than to set about the unrewarding inch-by-inch task of doing it. Poverty reform is a highly complex task, which must be the product of courageous political leadership and sophisticated planning; it must use methods which will allow the underprivileged to help themselves, and, insofar as professionals and quasi-professionals may be needed, methods which ensure that people who need assistance will not simply be dumped from agency to agency and bureaucracy to bureaucracy.

We do need a juvenile court to prosecute youngsters charged with serious criminal offenses, to assist in resolving the problems of adolescents who can no longer live at home, and to review charges of serious physical or emotional child-abuse. But cases in which the courts are merely used as a club to enforce the views of middle-class social workers and inept regulations should be no part of a judicial system. Another reason to insist upon a rather narrow jurisdiction for a family court is to prevent some of the dumping. The juvenile court too often acts as a rubber stamp, giving its imprimatur to the switching of children and families from agency to agency. Yet, if we examine the lives of the people described in this book, I believe it is safe to say that probably 90 per cent of them should never have been brought within the ambits of the juvenile justice system in the first place.

For instance, the problems of Lottie Ervin, the lady whose children were taken away from her because there was not enough food in the home, could not be resolved by a court system. Similarly, Monica Voigt's appalling difficulties in attempting to raise three children on welfare and at the same time to advance herself so that her children could have a better life, were the result of a stupid welfare system that rewards those who are content to recycle their barren lives from generation to generation, and punishes those who would attempt to better themselves. Her problems were equally the result of a blind school system that regards education only as a nine-to-five, seven-through-sixteen mandate to be shed as quickly as possible.

Where in all of this is a sensible day-care center or an adult-education class?

Lastly, consider the problems of Matilda McIntosh and her voyage through Illinois' various bureaucracies and agencies. If she did have certain emotional problems related to her intellectual brilliance and extreme poverty, the schools should have provided therapy and advanced schooling for her. But ghetto children are not supposed to be brilliant, so there are no classes for superior children in most inner-city schools. When the school system felt it could not help her, they sent her on to a private agency. When the social workers there decided they were powerless, they dumped her on the Juvenile Court, which in turn rerouted Matilda and her mother to the DCFS. While with the DCFS she was sent to an orphanage and three foster homes before the caseworkers gave up on her and put her with the DHM. She was with Mental Health for a year before *those* workers shipped her off to the DOC, where she remained for almost three years. Quite obviously, there was nothing the court could do or did do to help Matilda, but as long as there was always another agency, the court could let the bureaucrats mandated to care for her simply say, She is beyond our help, and shove her off to someone else.

A huge proportion, then, of the so-called problems of which I have written could have been resolved in a flexible and responsive school system. It would seem that the most sensible way to provide adequate educational services in large urban areas is to break down any huge central system into many smaller boards of education elected by local communities, but keeping a central curriculum office. However, the educational establishment is opposed to this and raises the shibboleth of racism in arguing against it. A community school system, the argument goes, would tend to become the weapon of the worst aspects of any one community. In black communities racism against whites would be taught, and in white communities the opposite. Yet the big school boards in our cities today *are not teaching,* and alternatives must be found.* There are so many services a flexible school system could bring to a community—including day care, adequate meals, adult education, family counseling and therapy, recreational activities, as well as the basic educational curriculum. It really is a question not so much of funds as of flexibility. And, unfortunately, the schools today carry out their wooden, inflexible, noneducative tasks at a very expensive rate to taxpayers and students.

Crucial to the prevention of the dumping of poor people from agency to agency on one hand, and on the other of providing (as inexpensively as possible to the taxpayers) a way out of the slums for disadvantaged citizens, is a central planning system by which that portion of the tax dollar set aside for such purposes is allotted rationally. Federal, state, and city tax funds and, now, revenue-sharing funds are funneled to several agencies in any one community—mental health, education, welfare, services for neglected and delinquent children, etc.—without regard to rational use. Each bureaucracy fights with the others and with the federal agencies, state legislatures, and city halls for their share of the tax dollar. (It seems to be in the nature of bureaucracies to grab all the money they can so as to expand into as many areas as possible.) In the meantime, the agencies giving the money may investi-

*The Chicago public-school system is the second largest in the nation, with a population of about 500,000 students. In 1971, 62 per cent of the children entering first grade were prepared for it, as compared against a national average of 69 per cent. But by eighth grade, kids were scoring in reading at only the 35 percentile level nationally. What makes this regressive situation so bleak for the poor population is that while 72 per cent of eighth-graders in predominantly white schools were reading above the national average, only five schools in the black and other minority communities reached or bettered that medium. Worse, the schools are not only not educating but doing so expensively. The Chicago Board of Education spent almost $30 million to operate its central office in 1971–72. On the other hand, the fourth largest school system in the nation—Chicago's parochial Catholic school system, with a population of approximately 250,000 students in primarily community-organized schools—spent only $600,-000 for the same purpose.

gate or monitor the bureaucracy getting the money but do nothing to determine whether or not the services offered by each of the many bureaucracies overlap.

For instance, in one small Chicago neighborhood there are three community mental-health centers funded by federal, state, and local funds. Each of these vies with the others as to which is the most effective for the community, while the common consensus is that all three exist primarily for the people who are employed at them. None considers its function to be that of giving individual therapy or counseling for people who live in the neighborhood. Entire books could be written about the tremendous waste and cost to the taxpayers of supporting Ph.D.s who talk about problems in poor communities while doing nothing to alleviate them.

Each bureaucracy whose task it is to give services to disadvantaged citizens is responsible to various budgetary offices, such as a comptroller or budget bureau. But these offices do not usually have central planning programs with criteria for determining what resources should be placed into which areas. This is a disgrace. The needs of the people are too important to be left to the discretion of nine or ten bureaucracies, each jealously clinging to its power enclaves and fighting with each other over resources which very often are overlapping and wasted.

Citizens who are supposed to be assisted by the state must have some form of power over it. Many of the inequities caused to our clients were the result of irrational decisions made by lower-level state bureaucrats and stupidly upheld by their superiors. Of course, we had many of these decisions reversed, but only after expensive and time-consuming litigation. And we only represented a few of the people who had been kicked around. The political system itself once compensated for these errors, and was able to direct the bureaucracies to be more sensitive to the needs of those for whom they were set up. But we seem to have reached a stage now where the bureaucracies run themselves without regard to political or public pressure of any sort.

Smaller nations have developed ombudsman systems to short-circuit bureaucratic intransigency. This middle man between the citizen and the state bureaucracy processes complaints and has the power to inspect records, call for hearings, and either insist on relief at his own word or use the courts to bring about equity. Such a system connected to a central planning board would have a great deal more power: while processing citizen complaints, it would also be evaluating the bureaucracies and be in a position to influence their decisions through their control of the budget.

Although the problems I have described in this book are complex ones, possible solutions are known, well chronicled, and to a great extent merely a matter of common sense. The major factor which has been lacking to date is courageous, innovative, and creative political leadership. Because a system or bureaucracy worked at one time does not mean that it will work today. And we need political leaders who will say so. The people, and the men and women they elect to represent them, must search the present state bureaucracies to determine which must be eradicated, which changed, and which combined. However, the political climate too often combines radical rhetoric (whether conservative or liberal-radical is irrelevant) with *status quo* actions, the emphasis being put on staying in office and keeping the other guy out, rather than on achievement. To the extent there is achievement, it is accomplished in the most visible manner, like building highways and stadiums, rather than rethinking and rebuilding a structure that will take a long time and cannot be seen.

TO SIT in a Legal Aid office day in and day out and see the various stages of *homo Americanus pauverus* can be a deeply depressing experience. *Oedipus* solved the riddle of who first crawls on all fours, then walks on two feet, and lastly on three legs; it was man. In our office we saw the modern equivalent of that riddle every day. We talked to the wild, untamed, frightened, street-wise, street-raised child. We spent days with swaggering, defiant, but equally frightened adolescents. And, saddest of all, we tried to help Chicago's disheartened middle-aged and older men and women. Hemingway once wrote that good men are sometimes broken in many places by society but that, being strong, they mend in the broken places and are often the better for it. He must have been talking about the average middle-class man or an unusually strong person. The older people we interviewed were broken in too many places too often, and could not arrest their decline into so much spiritual pulp. Indeed, if it were possible for them to mend at all, it would perhaps be even more heartbreaking; because for every broken place they could mend, there were ten new broken places.

One day a man in his fifties came to the office to see me while I was busy finishing a brief. I told the secretary I could not talk to him and to ask him to make an appointment. But he literally begged to see me, and so I impatiently relented. He was in his fifties, though he looked perhaps ten years older. He was black. When he addressed me, his voice shook almost as much as his hands, and I could see that he felt he was somehow in the presence of someone better and more important than he. He told me a story. His son, who was at St. Charles, the medium-security jail, had been shot three times by police when he was apprehended in a burglary. Apparently, one of the bullets had lodged in his spine and left him a cripple. The boy had been jailed for eight months, and his mother had been physically and mentally ill ever since. The father was beside himself with grief, and beseeched me to help. His son, he said pathetically, had sure paid the price for his youthful recklessness with three bullets in his back.

I told him I would do something, but in my mind I could not determine what it would be. As he continued to talk, I lost the sense of what he was saying, and it became a jumble of words all of which I had heard a thousand times before. In my mind, I kept thinking of Larry Woodson's testimony at the Sheridan trial. "I've been tired for the longest, I've been tired for the longest, I've been tired for the longest."

APPENDIX

The following appendix includes citations of a few of the cases listed in this book. For the most part, I have included only the initial of the person's last name to protect the anonymity of the individual. Where appropriate, I have included the name I used in the book in parentheses.

1. Rights of Unwed Fathers to Their Children
   Stanley v. *Illinois,* 92 So. Ct. 1208
2. Cases Involving Constitutionality of Incarceration of Runaways
   V., et al. v. *Scott and Hanrahan,* 467 F2d 1235 (No. 71–1387)
   In re S., 48 Ill. 2d 431; 270 N.E. 2d 7 (1971) (Miromir)
3. Cases Involving Constitutionality of Neglect Statute
   In re S., Appellate Court of Illinois (1st Dist.), No. 58537
   W., et al. v. *Scott, et al.* (72 C 1112 U.S.D.C., No. Dist. Ill.)
4. Sheridan Cases
   In re O., et al. (Cir. Ct. of Cook County, 70 J 18495)
   W., et al. v. *Bensinger, et al.* (71–1385 U.S. Dist. Ct.)
   U.S., ex. rel. S., et al. v. *Coughlin* (U.S. Dist. Ct. Nos. 71 C 1792–1795); 472 F2d 100
5. Audy Home Cases
   P., et al. v. *Laymon, et al.* (72 C 766, U.S.D.C., No. Dist. Ill.)
6. Cases Involving Right of Child to Sue State Agency for Violation of Constitutional Rights
   W., et al. v. *Glass* (7th Cir., No. 71–1677); 473 F2d 983 (Armstrong)
   W. v. *Weaver, et al.* (7th Cir., No. 71–1679); *Per Curiam* Decision in U.S. Court of Appeals (McIntosh)
7. Rights of Child to Hearing Upon Commitment to Mental Health Facility and Appointment of Our Office as Attorney for This Class of Children
   In re L., et al. (Cir. Ct. Cook County, Juv. Div., No. 68 J 15805)
8. Unconstitutionality of Transfer to Chester
   N. v. *Glass, et al.* (Cir. Ct. Cook County, County Div., No. 72 Co. NMT 2635) (Crane)
9. Racial Discrimination of Private Child Care Facilities
   In re F., et al. (Cir. Ct. Cook County, No. 65 FCD 7665)
10. Texas Institutions-Related Cases
    In re B., et al. (Cir. Ct. Cook County, 71 J 4128)
    In re G., et al. (Cir. Ct. Cook County, No. 64 FCD 3139, 68 J 13133)
11. Proper Medical Care of State Wards
    In re C. (Denise) v. *Jerome Miller, et al.* (Nos. 68 J 15417, 70 J 1435)
12. Freedom of Speech—Press
    (Brad Stewart) v. *Laymon* (73 C 651, Civil Rights, U.S. Dist. Ct., N.D. Ill.)